HOW TO
WRITE A PAPER

Five Steps
to Writing a Theological
or Literary Research Paper

ANDREW DAVID NASELLI

"Naselli's book helpfully supplies students a step-by-step, uncomplicated guide to writing a research paper, and by this he supplies teachers greater joys in grading and mobilizing a new generation of faithful communicators."

—**Jason S. DeRouchie**, Research Professor of Old Testament and Biblical Theology and Rich and Judy Hastings Endowed Chair of Old Testament Studies, Midwestern Baptist Theological Seminary; Pastor, Sovereign Joy Baptist Church in Kansas City, Missouri

"This is a remarkable resource that I wish I'd had on my desk years ago. As valuable for a professor as for a student, it is a practical guide to that dread academic exercise: the writing and the grading of research papers. It covers everything from conception to completion: researching and outlining, documenting and reasoning, editing and honing. I am buying copies for all my teachers."

—**George Grant**, pastor of Parish Presbyterian Church (PCA) in Franklin, Tennessee; founder of Franklin Classical School, the Chalmers Fund, and the King's Meadow Study Center; author of more than 70 books

"Andy Naselli is one of the most enjoyable authors to read because his prose is so clear and his style unencumbered by the typical academic jargon of our day. This book gives you direct insight on his writing process. Not only that, Naselli demonstrates what is the true foundation of clear writing—namely, clear thinking. Students and professors will gain practical, actionable insights for their academic writing and grading. Our day is in need of coherent and logical arguments made in a way that is faithful to God's word and comprehensible to readers. That is where impact is made. I am grateful for the way this book paves the way for such writing to take place."

—**Jeremy M. Kimble**, Professor of Systematic and Applied Theology, Cedarville University

"Professors often jest (with that kernel of truth that every good joke contains) that we teach for free and are paid to grade. Poorly researched, badly argued, sloppily written papers are to blame, of course, but the sad fact is that far too many papers match this description. And while only the gifts of God can make a great writer, anyone can become a good writer—or, at least, a *better* one. Naselli shows the way as a man who is no stranger to the author's pen, having written two dissertations and a full shelf of books. Wise is the student who follows his advice, and blessed is the professor who makes this book required reading in his classes."

—**Doug Ponder**, Academic Dean and Professor of Biblical Studies, Grimké Seminary; Teaching Pastor, Remnant Church in Richmond, Virginia

"Professors know the joys of teaching. Students know the joys of learning. And both professors and students know the pains of grading. In *How to Write a Paper*, Andy Naselli aims to increase joy and relieve pain for professors and students alike. Clearly and succinctly, he guides the reader through the research-and-writing process, modeling careful thinking, discipline, and pastoral wisdom. Practical and easy to read, this needed work will benefit every student looking to improve his research and writing. I heartily recommend it!"

—**Michael Riccardi**, Assistant Professor of Theology, The Master's Seminary; Pastor of Local Outreach Ministries, Grace Community Church in Sun Valley, California

"Like Dr. Naselli, I'm a professor who teaches for free and gets paid to grade. And I'm always on the lookout for resources to help students with the writing process. Dr. Naselli has written an accessible guide for both students and teachers. It will aid students in research and writing, and it will bless teachers with better papers. Read it, and then get to writing."

—**Joe Rigney**, Fellow of Theology and Director of Greyfriars Hall, New Saint Andrews College; Associate Pastor, Christ Church in Moscow, Idaho

"In a world so often confusing and needlessly complicated, full of ambiguity and conflicting authorities shouting each other down, it is a profound relief to have someone sit you down and explain in a kind, clear voice exactly what is expected and why. This book speaks to you as if you were a slightly panicked student grasping at straws, and it offers you a life-raft of sound, plain-spoken advice, with helpful tables and examples. Read it."

—**Carson Spratt**, Rhetoric and Integrated Humanities Teacher, Logos Online School (https://LogosOnlineSchool.com)

"This short book presents clear, practical, step-by-step help for students writing research papers. Naselli is a seasoned writer, editor, and teacher, and here he offers wise counsel applicable to anyone who wants to write well."

—**Brian J. Tabb**, President and Professor of Biblical Studies, Bethlehem College and Seminary; General Editor, *Themelios*

"Writing research papers does not come naturally to any of us. We need expert guidance, and Andy Naselli's short work may be the best concise one-stop shop for students to get started. If used well, it should result in clearer writing, better thinking, and happier teachers."
—**Justin Taylor**, Executive Vice President of Book Publishing and Book Publisher, Crossway; Managing Editor, *The ESV Study Bible*

"Unfortunately, in our current educational system and the age of social media, the skill of how to write a solid research paper is becoming a lost art. This is why I am thrilled to recommend Andy Naselli's *How to Write a Paper*. Naselli covers the crucial points with helpful illustrations regarding how to write an excellent paper, which will greatly aid students and receive the thanks of many teachers. Simply a wonderful resource for students of all ages and educational backgrounds."
—**Stephen J. Wellum**, Professor of Christian Theology, The Southern Baptist Theological Seminary; Editor, *The Southern Baptist Journal of Theology*; Pastor, Providence Baptist Church in Sellersburg, Indiana

"Andy Naselli has given students a gift: a guide that helps them steward their written words. Clear, practical, and accessible, this book trains students to write with patience and precision. Those who take its counsel seriously will not only write better papers—they will become better communicators."
—**Jonathon Woodyard**, Vice President of Student Life and Assistant Professor of Historical Theology, Southwest Baptist University

HOW TO WRITE A PAPER

Five Steps
to Writing a Theological
or Literary Research Paper

ANDREW DAVID NASELLI

BUILD & FIGHT PRESS
LAKE ELMO, MINNESOTA

Andrew David Naselli, *How to Write a Paper:*
Five Steps to Writing a Theological or Literary Research Paper.
Published by Build & Fight Press.
Lake Elmo, Minnesota.
Copyright ©2026 by Andrew David Naselli.
All rights reserved.
http://www.AndyNaselli.com/.

Cover design by Boaz Prince.
Interior design by Andrew David Naselli and Boaz Prince.

All italics in Bible quotations are added.

Format (e.g., abbreviations for theological journals or for books of the Bible) follows *The SBL Handbook of Style: For Biblical Studies and Related Disciplines*, 2nd ed. (Atlanta: SBL Press, 2014).

Hardcover ISBN: 979-8-9946480-0-1
E-book ISBN: 979-8-9946480-1-8

Library of Congress Cataloging-in-Publication Data is on file with the publisher.

To my seminary students:

It is a joy to teach you how the five theological disciplines—
exegesis,
biblical theology,
historical theology,
systematic theology,
and practical theology—
interrelate and culminate in doxology.

I hope it will also be a joy to grade the next batch of research papers.

Table of Contents

Expanded Table of Contents

6 Introductory Questions

Question 1. Who is this book for?

This book is for *students*.

I prepared the book particularly for students at Bethlehem College and Seminary in Minneapolis. Our students study the Bible and the Great Books of Western Civilization—works of history, literature, philosophy, and theology that have stood the test of time and that have resonated with mankind through the ages and around the world.

This book would be most helpful in other institutions at the level of college and graduate school. Advanced high school students could use it as well.

Question 2. How should you use this book?

This book can save you a lot of grief.

- If you are a student, read this little book straight through before you write a paper, and consult it along the way as you plan, research, write, and revise. That will save you a lot of grief because it will help you know what to do.

- If you are a teacher, require your students to read this little book before they begin the paper-writing process. That may save you a lot of grief because few tasks irritate professors more than grading poor-quality papers.

This book is about how to write a *research paper*, but the principles apply to shorter essays as well as longer works such as an MA thesis, ThM thesis, DMin thesis, or PhD dissertation.

Question 3. Why did I write this book?

I'll admit it: I wrote this book because I don't like grading poorly written papers. I figured that my students would write better papers if I prepared an accessible how-to manual for them.

When it's paper-grading crunch time at the end of a semester, sometimes I have to fight the sin of grumpiness. My mindset as a professor is that I teach for free and get paid to grade (plus attend administrative meetings). I don't love grading papers when they are full of poorly researched content, half-baked arguments, and distracting errors in grammar, style, and format.[1]

But I didn't write this book just for me. I wrote it for *my fellow teachers* because I feel their pain—with *tethered* empathy, of course.[2] And I wrote it for *my students* because I genuinely care about them.

Students, learning to *write* and learning to *think* go together. The better you get at one, the better you'll get at the other. This little how-to book is my gift to you so that your papers can be a delight to your professors and anyone else who reads them. It's refreshing when a paper is a delight to read: well-researched content + strong arguments + proper grammar and format + an elegant style. That's like a cool breeze on a hot afternoon.

---

[1] When I shared a draft of this book with John Piper (founder and chancellor of Bethlehem College and Seminary), he replied with an interesting anecdote from his days as a seminary student: "This reminded me of Dan Fuller, who had us seminary beginners read his paper 'How to Write a Book Review' before we wrote a paper about a book he assigned. He no doubt had similar frustrations as yours. Interestingly, he graded our papers with an audio recording using 5.6, for example, to indicate six tenths of the way down page five. This was before cell phones, and he did it on a big Wollensak reel-to-reel tape recorder and told each of us what time stamp our critique was on, and we had to make an appointment to listen to it in his receptionist's office. I hope your guidance helps produce good thinkers and good writers, which are almost the same thing" (email from John Piper to Andy Naselli, 11 July 2025, shared with permission).

[2] In case you missed the joke, see Joe Rigney, *The Sin of Empathy: Compassion and Its Counterfeits* (Moscow, ID: Canon, 2025).

Question 4. Why does this book focus on a *theological* or *literary* research paper?

This book is not a how-to manual for how to write any and every kind of research paper. Research papers for technical fields like chemistry and math are different. I am focusing on a *theological* or *literary* research paper because that is the type of research paper that students write at my school. I teach systematic theology, biblical theology, New Testament, and ethics. The principles I teach in this book also apply to writing research papers on literature other than the Bible such as Plato, Shakespeare, and Lewis.

Question 5. How does it benefit you to work hard at writing a research paper?

Many students would answer, "I'd get a better grade." It's true that you will likely earn a better grade if you work hard to improve at writing a research paper. And that is a legitimate motivation.

But if that is your *primary* motivation, then you have a problem. Your problem is that you care too much about your grades and too little about the purpose of education. The purpose of education is not to get a degree with a high GPA. The purpose of education is to equip and enculturate you to glorify God in all of life. Letter grades like A, B, and C are simply tools to evaluate how well you are doing.

A grade can seem really important to you at the time you receive it, but years down the road, nobody cares. What matters is what kind of *person* you are. What matters is that you love God with your entire being and that you love your neighbor as yourself. Working hard to improve at writing a research paper helps you become a better all-around person. (This issue is a subset of how getting a liberal arts education helps you become a better all-around person.[3])

---

[3] See Joe Rigney, "Broad Minds and Big Hearts: A Case for Christian Liberal-Arts Education," *Desiring God*, 21 February 2019, https://www.desiringgod.org/articles/broad-minds-and-big-hearts. Doug Wilson

Chick-fil-A is a fantastic place for a young person to work because it trains you to excel at outstanding *customer service*. The skill of cheerfully and responsibly assisting people is transferable to just about every domain of life. Working at Chick-fil-A can train you to be a better all-around person.

In a similar way, working hard to improve at writing a research paper can make you a better all-around person. How so? You can benefit in at least seven ways. (More precisely, you can better *glorify God* or make much of God in these seven ways.)

Benefit 1. You can think more clearly and deeply.

The process of writing a research paper trains you to think clearly and deeply.[4] The process of writing is the most fruitful way to clarify what I think about something—especially a complex topic. Walter Hooper, who served as C. S. Lewis's secretary, recounts,

---

shows how a liberal arts education connects to writing: "If you are in a position to do so, which usually means that you are young enough, make sure to get a thorough and broad liberal arts education. I am astonished at how many young Christians want to be writers and how few of them want to mess with all the prerequisites, which look suspiciously to them like work. A good liberal arts education will acquaint you, like it or not, with a broad spectrum of writing genres, and as you are working through them, try your hand at writing your own. It also provides grist for the mill—you know enough to have something to say. If you took a number of average nineteen-year-olds who want to be writers and said, 'Great, here's a contract,' and then asked them what was on their mind, what they had to say, many of them would have to say that their sole insight is that they want to be a writer." Douglas Wilson, *Wordsmithy: Hot Tips for the Writing Life* (Moscow, ID: Canon, 2011), 67.

[4] When one of my former seminary students read a draft of this book, he shared this feedback: "My subheading for this book would be *or, How to Learn and Think Well*. I think there is a substantial miss on the marketable value of this book by linking the book's content only with paper writing. It seems to me that your primary point in all of these sections is not just how to write a paper well but teaching students how good paper writing is meant to form the foundation for serious learning and intellectual growth. You teach these things well in this book. I would read this book post-school to learn those things. I would have more likely read this book in school to learn those things than merely for knowing how to get a good grade on a paper (which is what your title suggests to me)."

I once asked how he [i.e., C. S. Lewis] managed to write with such ease, and I think his answer tells us more about his writing than anything he said. He told me that the thing he most loved about writing was that it did two things at once. This he illustrated by saying: 'I don't know what I *mean* till I see what I've *said*.' In other words, writing and thinking were a single process.[5]

Writing helps you clarify what you think. *Reading, conversing,* and *writing* go together to make you a well-rounded person. Philosopher Francis Bacon explains,

Reading maketh a full man, conference [i.e., conversation] a ready man, and writing an exact man. And therefore, if a man write little, he had need have a great memory; if he confer [i.e., converse] little, he had need have a present wit; and if he read little, he had need have much cunning to seem to know that he doth not.[6]

When you *read* deeply, that copiousness overflows in conversations. *Conversing* about what you read helps you clarify what you think about it and helps you communicate easily and promptly. *Writing* about what you read forces you to clarify *more precisely* what you think about it.[7]

John Piper explains, "In one sense, publishing is secondary to my writing. If nobody wanted to read what I write, I would still write, because it's how I see things, and how I savor reality. It's how I learn."[8] When you write a paper, you can't simply dictate a jumble

---

[5] Walter Hooper, preface to vol. 3 of C. S. Lewis, *The Collected Letters of C. S. Lewis*, ed. Walter Hooper, 3 vols. (San Francisco: HarperSanFrancisco, 2004–2007), 3:xvi (italics in original).

[6] Francis Bacon, *The Essays: or, Counsels Civil and Moral*, 7th ed. (London: Routledge, 1891), 267–68.

[7] This paragraph updates Andrew David Naselli, *How to Read a Book: Advice for Christian Readers* (Moscow, ID: Canon, 2024), 63.

[8] John Piper, *Reading the Bible Supernaturally: Seeing and Savoring the Glory of God in Scripture* (Wheaton, IL: Crossway, 2017), 413.

of unprocessed words with a speech-to-text program and leave it at that. You must carefully choose what words to use. You draft words and revise them. When you excel at this process, then you will excel at thinking more clearly. And when you think more clearly, you can better understand reality—the reality of God's *word* and the reality of God's *world*.

Benefit 2. You can communicate more clearly and concisely.

The process of writing a research paper trains you to communicate more clearly and concisely (especially when your paper has a word limit). That skill is important for all of life—whether you are talking to a family member or sending a text message or writing an email or advising a friend or trying to win an argument or teaching a class or preaching a sermon or writing a paper.

When you excel at the skill of writing clearly about a complicated topic, you become better at communicating clearly with just about anybody. If you can accurately and clearly write about Trinitarian heresies, then you are better equipped to helpfully answer questions about the Trinity from a seven-year-old girl or a Muslim Uber driver or a skeptic who lives next door.

Benefit 3. You can more fairly evaluate opposing arguments.

John Piper describes education as instilling six habits of mind and heart.[9] Here's my paraphrase:[10]

1. *Observe accurately and thoroughly.* Are you seeing what is actually there in the text?

---

[9] See John Piper, Foundations for Lifelong Learning: Education in Serious Joy (Wheaton, IL: Crossway, 2023).
[10] This is from Naselli, *How to Read a Book*, 39.

2. *Understand what you observe clearly.* Are you perceiving what the author intended to communicate?

3. *Evaluate what you have understood fairly.* Is it true and valuable?

4. *Feel that evaluation intensely and proportionately.* Are your emotions in accord with the truth and worth of what you have observed, understood, and evaluated? "Abhor what is evil; hold fast to what is good" (Rom 12:9). Hate what God hates, and love what God loves.

5. *Apply your discoveries to all of life wisely and helpfully.* So what? Why does it matter?

6. *Express your discoveries compellingly.* Can you communicate what you have observed, understood, evaluated, felt, and applied in a way that others can know and enjoy that accuracy, clarity, truth, value, and helpfulness?

People often skip over *observing* and *understanding* and jump straight to *evaluating*. Or worse, they jump straight to *feeling* and *expressing*. They just *emote*. When you learn to write an outstanding research paper, you learn to observe accurately and thoroughly, to understand clearly, and *then* to evaluate fairly.

Developing this skill is like focusing on the four main compound lifts for strength training: squat, deadlift, press, and bench press. Those lifts train *functional* movements that you use in everyday life—like picking up groceries off the ground or lifting a carryon suitcase above your seat on an airplane. It's practical. It's a skill you'll use daily because it is basic to doing normal activities. In a similar way, the skill of evaluating opposing arguments fairly is practical. It's a skill you'll use daily because it is basic to thinking and communicating.

A bonus of learning to fairly evaluate an opposing argument is that it can help you overcome being emotionally brittle and prone to anxiety if you encounter a contrary opinion. (It may also convince you to change your mind.) You can learn to analyze aggressive and incisive arguments and to improve your own views.[11]

Benefit 4. You can better affirm and love what is true, good, and beautiful, and you can better refute and hate what is false, evil, and ugly.

When you can think and communicate more clearly, you can better affirm what is actually true, good, and beautiful (like God's design for men and women), and you can better refute what is actually false, evil, and ugly (like feminism or LGBT ideology). You can better love what God loves and hate what God hates. You can develop personal positions and convictions on controversial topics. Clarity is so much better than a hazy, fuzzy, smoky confusion.

It's like you're sitting in the chair at an eye-exam, and the eye doctor asks you to look through a bunch of lenses. When you look through some lenses, you can't see a thing. Everything is fuzzy. But when you look through the lenses that end up as your new prescription, ah! Clarity. Precision. The right lenses are satisfying and tension-relieving. The process of writing a research paper can train you to cultivate that kind of clarity and precision for all of life.

Benefit 5. You can better influence others.

When you can think and communicate more clearly, then you can better influence others. It is unusual for a person to be able both to *see* clearly and to *explain* clearly to others what he sees. A person with that skill set is better equipped to influence others—to influence them to affirm and love what is true, good, and beautiful and to refute and hate what is false, evil, and ugly. You can better influence

---

[11] Thanks to Josh Sullivan, my former Teaching Assistant at Bethlehem Seminary, for suggesting the insight in this paragraph.

others with your words in private communication, in public speaking, and in writing—whether a text message or a research paper.

Years ago one of my students was having a hard time in one of my classes because I kept suggesting ways that he could write more clearly and concisely. He was initially discouraged, but he kept at it and got better. A few years later he thanked me for coaching him to write better. He shared that he was getting promoted at work because his superiors valued his skill to communicate clearly and concisely when he wrote emails.

Benefit 6. You can better cultivate the virtue of self-control.

Proverbs 25:28 says, "A man without self-control / is like a city broken into and left without walls." To have self-control means that your passions don't master you. You are not enslaved to your passions. The Holy Spirit strongly influences you, and you increasingly bear the fruit of the Spirit.

Self-control is a virtue you should cultivate, and the hard work of writing a research paper can train you to better cultivate that virtue. The same goes for strength training or sprinting. It's good for you to do hard things. It trains you to have self-control.

Benefit 7. You can more faithfully steward the skills God has entrusted to you.

The Christian life is hard work. You must fight like a soldier. You must run and box like an athlete. You are responsible to work hard. You are responsible to be faithful with what God has given you.

If you are a student with the responsibility to write a research paper, then you are responsible to work hard at writing a research paper. God has given you the ability to think and read and study and argue, and now you are responsible to cultivate the skills God has entrusted to you. Improve. Get better. Pursue excellence. Yield an increase. Let's go!

Question 6. What are the steps to write an outstanding theological or literary research paper?

In the rest of this book, I break down the paper-writing process into five steps:

1. *Understand the assignment.* Know where you are trying to go before you start the journey.

2. *Plan ahead.* Prepare far in advance so that you complete your research paper well before the deadline.

3. *Choose your approach.* Prove a thesis (deductive), or explore a problem (inductive).

4. *Research and write.* Draft the paper.

5. *Revise.* Polish the cannonball.

Step 4 is the big one, so most of this book explains that step. But all five steps are important.

Step 1. Understand the Assignment:
Know where you are trying to go before you start the journey.

Here are three tips.

Tip 1. Pay attention to the required topic, word count, and format.

For example, for each of my three systematic theology courses, I require students to write a research paper. Here's what I say in my syllabus:

> Write a 3,500–5,000-word research paper that addresses an issue directly related to this course. Skillfully apply what you learn from the required reading and class times. Specifically, answer the question, "What does the whole Bible teach about _____?" Use a systematic-theological method in accordance with my book *How to Understand and Apply the New Testament*. (This is not a historical theology paper or a biblical theology paper.) The word count includes footnotes; it excludes front matter (title page + table of contents) and back matter (appendices + bibliography). For style, abbreviations, and bibliography, follow *The SBL Handbook of Style*, 2nd ed. (2014).

The requirements clearly specify the topic, the word count, and the format. The topic for this theological research paper is relatively open-ended. There are *hundreds* of topics that a student could write on. I encourage students to write on topics that interest them and that they perceive are relevant for their current or future ministries. But they must write a *systematic theology* paper—not another kind of paper:

- It is not primarily an *exegetical* paper, which carefully interprets the Bible by analyzing what the authors intended to communicate. For example, what does "she will be saved through childbearing" mean in 1 Tim 2:15? Of course, a systematic theology paper should do exegesis, but it should do more. It should *correlate* exegesis of related passages to show how the whole Bible coheres.

- It is not primarily a *biblical theology* paper, which studies how the whole Bible progresses, integrates, and climaxes in Christ. For example, trace the *temple* theme through the Bible's storyline. A systematic theology should incorporate some degree of biblical theology, but it should do more.

- It is not primarily a *historical theology* paper, which surveys and evaluates how significant exegetes and theologians have understood the Bible and theology. For example, what is John Calvin's view of the Lord's Supper? A systematic theology should incorporate some degree of historical theology, but it should do more.

- It is not primarily a *practical theology* paper, which applies the other theological disciplines to yourself, the church, and the world. For example, what are strategies for fighting the sin of anxiety? Systematic theology should not be disconnected from practical theology, but its focus is correlating how the whole Bible coheres.

Those four other types of papers are worth writing *for other courses*—just not for my systematic theology courses. Students must use the methodology I explicitly require for this paper.

For my Ethics course, I require the students to write a research paper on a specific topic: "Write a 3,500–5,000-word position paper on divorce and remarriage." Every student writes on the same issue.

The lesson here is that you need to accurately understand what your professor is asking you to do. If you want to write a different kind of paper, you are free to ask permission for an exception. Your professor may give you permission to deviate from the assignment. But if you don't receive that permission, don't deviate from the assignment and write what you want to write.

Tip 2. Make sure your mindset from the outset is to make an academic argument, not to preach a sermon.

Sermons are important and valuable, but a research paper is not a sermon. They differ in two notable ways:

1. They differ in their *goals*. Both a sermon and a research paper aim to *teach*. But a sermon also aims to *exhort*. A research paper aims to *persuade* but not to exhort.

2. They differ in their *audiences*. A sermon typically heralds and applies God's words to a *general* audience—a broad group of people with different backgrounds, education levels, and ages. Everyone in the audience usually does not have specialized knowledge in a specific field.

In contrast, a research paper is an argument for a particular academic audience. For example, the research papers for my seminary courses assume that the audience knows Hebrew and Greek.

When you are preparing to write a paper, answer these questions: Who is my academic audience? How does what I write fit in the conversation that academics have been having for centuries?

Tip 3. If you're not sure what exactly the assignment is, then ask clarifying questions to your professor (or his teaching assistant).

If you're not sure what to do, then you are responsible to figure that out. The best way to gain clarity is to ask the professor to clarify what the assignment is. You should know where you are trying to go before you start the journey.

Step 2. Plan Ahead:
Prepare far in advance so that you complete your research paper well before the deadline.

Students often procrastinate. You might put off writing your paper until the last possible moment. You might calculate how long it will take you to complete it, and you might assume that you will have all of that time to finish the assignment right until the moment it is due. If the paper is due by 11:59pm, you might plan to submit it at 11:58pm. Yes, that's technically on time, but it's cutting it way too close.

Here are seven reasons to plan ahead—to prepare far in advance so that you complete your research paper well before the deadline.

Reason 1. You can benefit from the leaf mold of your mind.

How did J. R. R. Tolkien create *The Lord of the Rings*? He explains the process like this:

> One writes such a story not out of the leaves of trees still to be observed, nor by means of botany and soil-science; but it grows like a seed in the dark *out of the leaf-mould of the mind*: out of all that has been seen or thought or read, that has long ago been forgotten, descending into the deeps. No doubt there is much selection, as with a gardener: what one throws on one's personal compost-heap; and my mould is evidently made largely of linguistic matter.[12]

---

[12] One of Tolkien's biographers cites this quotation: Humphrey Carpenter, *Tolkien: A Biography* (Boston: Houghton Mifflin, 1977), 126 (italics added). I have been unable to locate this precise quotation in Tolkien's writings. I presume that Carpenter had access to some of Tolkien's unpublished writings. Here is a similar quotation from one of Tolkien's letters: "One's mind is, of course, stored with a 'leaf-mould' of memories (submerged) of names, and these rise up to the surface at times, and may provide with modification the bases of 'invented' names." J. R. R.

When you read widely and have stimulating conversations and carefully observe the world God created, your mind is like a compost pile of leaf mold. Your mind can be fertile soil for organic growth, but that takes time. You can't expedite this process.

When I am in the process of writing a book or article, my mind never fully disengages. If I take a physical break from writing, ideas for how to tweak what I'm writing spontaneously come to mind while I'm in the shower or making lunch or lying down to fall asleep. When that happens, I try to capture the idea in a note on my phone as quickly as possible before I lose it. Where do those ideas come from? I don't know how to explain the complex way that God designed our brains, but my guess is that Tolkien's leaf-mold metaphor is at least part of the answer.

Reason 2. You will be prepared if an emergency occurs.

Something always comes up:
- It's your friend's birthday.
- You accidentally fall asleep.
- You get sick.
- A family member or friend dies.
- Your car breaks down.
- Your basement floods.
- Your computer crashes.
- Your baby is born early.
- You get writer's block.
- A Philippian jailer asks you, "What must I do to be saved?"

And you miss the deadline.

Emergencies come up in life, and you should prepare for them by working ahead.

Tolkien, *The Letters of J. R. R. Tolkien*, ed. Humphrey Carpenter (Boston: Houghton Mifflin, 1981), 409 ("324 From a letter to Graham Tayar 4–5 June 1971").

Reason 3. You won't stress out your family.

As best I can recall, in over two decades of marriage, my wife and children have never known a stressful time when I had to hole up somewhere and miss family time because of a deadline. They have never felt the pressure of a looming deadline for Daddy: "Oh, no. Daddy has a _____ due. Let's all get out of Daddy's way and pray that he makes the deadline." That's been the case for two PhD degrees, nearly thirty books, over a hundred articles, hundreds of sermons, and thousands of lectures. How? It's not complicated: With God's help, I plan ahead and plod.

Reason 4. You will have sufficient time to draft your paper.

Writing a research paper is not like heating up a ready-to-go-meal in a microwave oven. It's more like preparing a hearty meal that includes brisket slow-grilling on a smoker, beef stew slow-cooking in a crockpot, sourdough bread baking in an oven, and sweet potatoes and broccoli crisping in an air fryer.

One does not simply walk into Mordor, and one does not simply rush into a research paper. An outstanding research paper is the result of hours and hours of thinking and revising and tweaking. You need time to engage primary and secondary sources and to weigh arguments and counterarguments. If you cram the writing process into an all-nighter, then the result will be half-baked. It'd be like rushing the bread-baking process and ending up with a loaf that is burnt on the outside and doughy on the inside.

Reason 5. You will have sufficient time to revise your paper.

Another benefit of planning ahead is that you have time to revise your paper—the final step in the process (Step 5 below). If you are feverishly writing your paper right up to the deadline (or worse, *after* the deadline), then you don't have sufficient time to revise your paper.

- When you finish the first draft of your paper and put it down for a week or two, you have a fresh perspective when you come back to it and can make it even better.

- An invaluable part of improving your paper is to solicit feedback from others. But you can't do that if you don't leave sufficient time for others to read your paper and share thoughtful feedback.

Reason 6. It helps you avoid plagiarism.

The paper-writing process will become more rushed the closer you get to the deadline. Consequently, you may *unintentionally* plagiarize as a result of cutting corners under pressure. You may fail to take notes carefully or paraphrase accurately or cite sources properly.

Or worse, you may *intentionally* plagiarize. You may say to yourself, "I'll use just a little AI help to ideate and to generate some content that will help me get past writer's block." (See Appendices A and B on plagiarism and artificial intelligence.)

Reason 7. It is good training for life.

Planning ahead for your paper deadline is good training for life. If you are scheduled to preach a sermon on a Sunday morning, it is not a legitimate excuse to show up on that Sunday morning and say, "Sorry, brothers and sisters. I got behind on stuff, and I didn't prepare my sermon. Y'all pray for me!" You should be responsible by planning ahead. Be reliable. Be trustworthy. Be responsible.

* * * * * * *

You might be thinking, "OK, you've convinced me. I should plan ahead. But how?" For more specific advice on productivity and time management, see "Appendix D. Productivity: How should you manage your time so that you can write a good research paper?"

Step 3. Choose Your Approach:
Prove a thesis (deductive), or explore a problem (inductive).

It's important to choose how you approach your research paper so that your paper is coherent and focused. My mentor D. A. Carson taught me that there are two ways to approach writing a dissertation, and his advice applies to writing a research paper.[13] You can either *prove a thesis* or *explore a problem*. Let's compare those two approaches with four tables.

Fig. 1. Deductive and Inductive Approaches

Prove a thesis.	Explore a problem.
Deductive argument: Begin with a thesis—a statement or theory that you want to maintain or prove. Then systematically prove the thesis.	*Inductive argument:* Begin without a thesis because you're not certain what to argue. Instead, begin with a problem to explore. You want to examine the evidence to see what the truth is, and you aren't sure what you're going to find and what you're going to conclude. This approach is not aimless. You should arrive at a conclusion by the end. But you present the data differently. You are systematically investigating an issue to see where the evidence leads.

---

[13] Cf. Andrew David Naselli, "Don Carson's Advice about Two Ways to Approach Writing a Dissertation," *Thoughts on Theology*, 3 December 2007, http://andynaselli.com/don-carsons-advice-about-two-ways-to-approach-writing-a-dissertation.

Fig. 2. Sample Theses and Problems

Sample Theses (Deductive)	Sample Problems (Inductive)
• Calvinism accurately represents what the Bible teaches about God's meticulous sovereignty in choosing to save specific individuals before he created the world. • The logic of 1 Tim 2:11–14 applies to more than just the one narrow prohibition that a woman may not preach a sermon to a church as a pastor. • William Shakespeare and C. S. Lewis present the theme of envy in similar but distinct ways. • Keswick theology is wrong. (That is the thesis for my first PhD dissertation. I knew from the outset what I wanted to prove because I had already given the subject a lot of thought, and this was an opportunity to systematically make a case against the higher life view of progressive sanctification.)[14]	• What does the Bible teach about God's sovereignty in choosing to save specific individuals? • How should we apply 1 Tim 2:11–14? • How do William Shakespeare and C. S. Lewis present the theme of envy? • How does Paul use the OT in Rom 11:34–35? (I explored this problem inductively for my second PhD dissertation. I wasn't sure what I would discover, and I was delighted to discover that Paul uses Job and Isaiah typologically. I didn't anticipate discovering that connection when I decided to study the passage. I initially chose the topic because I love Rom 11:33–36 and wanted to understand it better.)[15]

---

[14] For an accessible version of my work, see Andrew David Naselli, *No Quick Fix: Where Higher Life Theology Came From, What It Is, and Why It's Harmful* (Bellingham, WA: Lexham, 2017).

[15] For a published version of this dissertation, see Andrew David Naselli, *From Typology to Doxology: Paul's Use of Isaiah and Job in Romans 11:34–35* (Eugene, OR: Pickwick, 2012).

Fig. 3. Strengths of Deductive and Inductive Approaches

Prove a thesis (deductive).	Explore a problem (inductive).
• *Focused.* Your task is straightforward: Defend a clear, concise, specific, arguable claim. This helps you research and write efficiently. • *Motivational.* If you are excited to demonstrate your thesis, then your task can be invigorating from the beginning. This creates momentum for research and writing. • *Persuasive.* A well-defended thesis is compelling.	• *Impartial.* Your conclusion is more likely to be fair, open-minded, and unbiased since you started out uncertain where the evidence would lead. • *Possibly groundbreaking.* You might discover an original insight. • *Possibly exciting.* Your task is to follow the evidence wherever it leads, and you are not sure what you will find. Investigating the evidence could be exhilarating.

Fig. 4. Weaknesses of Deductive and Inductive Approaches

Prove a thesis (deductive).	Explore a problem (inductive).
• *Possibly biased*. In your zeal to prove your thesis, you may overlook or downplay evidence that undermines or weakens your thesis. • *Possibly manipulative*. In your zeal to prove your thesis, you may tweak or cherry-pick evidence to fit your thesis. • *Possibly premature*. You might commit to a thesis before you have sufficiently studied a subject.	• *Possibly unfocused*. You may struggle to focus your research and end up writing a paper that is disorganized or too broad. • *Possibly unremarkable and boring*. You may invest a lot of time and work only to discover that there is not much to discover. For example, you might study a particular syntactical construction in the Greek NT only to confirm that the traditional view among grammarians is correct. You now have a lot of well-organized data but no groundbreaking discovery to share. • *Possibly too hard*. You may discover that the topic you chose to investigate is simply too challenging or too big. It will take you far more time than you have to reach a responsible conclusion.

I have presented these two approaches as two distinct ways to write a paper. But it's possible to combine the approaches in various ways. Nevertheless, one of the ways will be dominant, and it's helpful to decide from the outset which approach to take for your research paper.

You may begin with one approach and later choose to write your paper in the style of the other approach.

- You may begin with an inductive approach because you don't know what you should argue. But then after studying the matter, you become confident what the correct view is and then choose to present that by proving a thesis (deductive).

- Or you may begin with a deductive approach and later decide that it would be more interesting and persuasive to present the data inductively.

I require students in my systematic theology courses to write a research paper that answers the question "What does the whole Bible say about _____?" That is the research question. After a student selects a topic to write about (e.g., the eternal functional submission of the Son to the Father), he then needs to choose whether to deductively prove a thesis (e.g., EFS is wrong) or inductively explore a problem (e.g., how should we interpret passages that say the Son submits to the Father?).

For students in my ethics course, I choose the research question for them: "What does the whole Bible say about divorce and remarriage?" I select the topic, and the student must present his personal position on the topic. He needs to choose whether to approach the topic deductively (e.g., God sometimes permits divorce as well as remarriage after divorce) or inductively (e.g., how does the phrase "except for sexual immorality" fit with God's design for marriage to be permanent?).

Step 4. Research and Write:
Draft the paper.

Before you write, you need to *have something to say*. To have something to say, you need to *research*. Once you have something to say, you need to *say it well*.[16]

The people you most enjoy reading are not always the most intelligent people. You enjoy reading people who both *have something to say* and *say it well*.

This step takes the most work and time, so this section is the longest in the book. (It takes up about half of the book.) The research-and-write stage has six components:

1. *Research*. Systematically investigate the evidence to establish facts and conclusions.

2. *Organize the paper*. Build a skeleton you can put flesh on.

3. *Develop a coherent argument*. Sharpen your reasoning.

4. *Interact with contrary views*. Present and respond to the strongest opposing arguments.

5. *Write clearly and concisely*. Omit needless words.

6. *Use proper grammar, syntax, and format*. Remove distractions by mastering the mechanics.

---

[16] "I will tell you a secret. This is all there is to the writing art: *having something to say, and saying it well*." James Kilpatrick, *Fine Print: Reflections on the Writing Art* (Kansas City, MO: Andrews & McMeel, 1993), 66 (italics added).

These six components are interconnected, so I am not presenting them as six distinct steps. You don't complete one of these tasks and then move on to the next. Rather, you work on all six of them simultaneously. Sometimes you focus more on one component, but you are continually working on and refining all six. For example, you don't *complete* your research and *then* start writing. You continue to research as you write. You refine your writing as you keep on researching.

For two illustrations, see "Appendix E. The Research-and-Write Process: Two Examples." I share the process for two of my books: a commentary on 1 Corinthians and a book on predestination.

The six components of the research-and-write stage are interrelated as you research and write. You should be working on all six components to various degrees until you finish the draft of your research paper. The final step (Step 5) is to *revise* your paper. This step (Step 4) is where you draft the whole paper.

Now let's consider the six components of researching and writing.

Component 1. Research:
Systematically investigate the evidence to establish facts and conclusions.

Your goal when you research is to establish what is true, and that requires that you responsibly investigate the evidence. "In the broadest terms, we do research whenever we gather information to answer a question that solves a problem."[17] Researching for a paper requires a lot of reading. Here are nine tips.

Tip 1. Read at different levels.

Don't be a one-speed bicycle. You don't have to read everything thoroughly and slowly. You should develop the skill of knowing when to slow down and when to speed up. In my book *How to Read a Book*, I distinguish three levels of reading:

1. *Micro-read:* Rigorously observe, understand, and evaluate what you read.

2. *Macro-read:* Read every word, but move quickly to get the big picture.

3. *Survey:* Quickly and efficiently size up a book without reading every word.[18]

Tip 2. Start by micro-reading the most important and helpful sources.

You need to have something worth saying before you start writing a research paper, so you should begin by reading widely. A good way to start is to carefully read some resources that responsibly

---

[17] Wayne C. Booth, Gregory G. Colomb, and Joseph M. Williams, *The Craft of Research*, 3rd ed. (Chicago: University of Chicago Press, 2008), 10.

[18] Naselli, *How to Read a Book*, 44–64. For some of my lectures and Q&A about reading at different levels, see https://andynaselli.com/how-to-read-a-book-advice-for-christian-readers.

survey your topic—like portions of systematic theology textbooks. Then micro-read a handful of sources that are most important and helpful. If you don't know what those are, then check with your professor or other experts to get advice about where to start. As you read the most important sources, you may notice that they refer to other sources that may be worth tracking down as you continue to investigate a matter.

Tip 3. Prioritize primary sources.

If you are writing a paper that is interpreting the Bible, then prioritize the Bible's original languages and translations of the Bible. If you are writing a paper on an author like Augustine or John Calvin or Jonathan Edwards or Jane Austen or C. S. Lewis, then prioritize what those authors wrote. Think deeply about primary sources before you rush to secondary sources.

As much as possible, don't be a *second-hander* with sources. For example, if you are writing a research paper on the NT and you can read Greek, then you should exegete the Greek text. You are at a major disadvantage if you don't know Greek because you are relying more on translations and commentaries. Good translations and commentaries are excellent tools that you should be using, but Scott Hafemann is right: "One hour with the text is worth ten in secondary literature.… Knowing the biblical languages enables us to do something very few commentaries ever do: trace the flow of the argument of the text."[19] If you know Greek, you can be a first-hander rather than a second-hander.[20]

---

[19] Scott J. Hafemann, "The SBJT Forum: Is It Genuinely Important to Use the Biblical Languages in Preaching, Especially since There Are Many Excellent Commentaries and Pastors Will Never Attain the Expertise of Scholars?," *Southern Baptist Journal of Theology* 3.2 (1999): 88.

[20] This paragraph updates Andrew David Naselli, *How to Understand and Apply the New Testament: Twelve Steps from Exegesis to Theology* (Phillipsburg, NJ: P&R Publishing, 2017), 122. (A second edition of this book is forthcoming in 2027.)

Tip 4. Engage secondary sources.

As important as primary sources are, a paper that engages *only* primary sources is not a *research* paper.

- A research paper is not a personal Bible study that interacts with the Bible and nothing else.

- A research paper is not an essay of your thoughts on a Jane Austen novel but that interacts with no other sources.

A research paper is an *academic* paper, which means that it interacts with the academy. A research paper must engage secondary sources that represent the academy. That is what makes the paper *academic*.

Tip 5. Prioritize quality secondary sources.

A research paper must engage secondary sources but not just *any* secondary sources. They should be *quality* sources.

Research is not looking over some blog posts that come up in a Google search. *Research* is not learning about theology and literature on YouTube and podcasts. I am not against Googling or watching videos or listening to podcasts. That can be profitable. But that is not rigorous academic research. A research paper is an academic essay. It's not a popular-level "post" fit for social media. It's a structured, scholarly, in-depth, evidence-based analysis or argument on a specific topic, and you should support your argument by systematically investigating quality sources.

What counts as a quality secondary source? An academic book or article by a qualified author. I don't want to be a snooty elitist here, but as a *general* rule, it includes peer-reviewed academic journals and monographs published by academic presses and other reputable publishers. (A *monograph* is a detailed book on a specialized topic.) I concede that there is a lot of low-quality material in such publications, but those sources are typically more academically responsible than what you might find on a popular website.[21]

Tip 6. Use a sufficient number of sources.

Sometimes graduate students ask me what is the *minimum* number of sources they must use for a theological research paper. They expect me to say something like, "Use at least ten sources." I don't say that because requiring a minimum number of sources seems more fitting for beginners like high school students or early college students. Instead I say this: "Use as many sources as necessary to write an outstanding research paper."

The number of sources you need to write an outstanding research paper depends on your topic and your argument and the nature of your sources. A relatively narrow topic with a straightforward argument may require fewer sources (perhaps only 10–15 sources), and an interdisciplinary topic with a complex argument may require more sources (perhaps 25–30 sources). It depends. If you're not sure if you are using a sufficient number of sources, ask your professor if he would advise you to read particular sources that you have not yet consulted. (And ask well before the paper is due!)

Fred Zaspel, a pastor-theologian, agrees that it is important to use a sufficient number of resources: "My own practice has been to read as widely and as deeply on the subject at hand as possible. Of course you must be discerning—don't waste your time reading fluff. But I want to read and read and read until I am no longer finding anything new."[22]

---

[21] In each course syllabus that I prepare for my seminary students, I end with a detailed bibliography that I have organized by topic. I am constantly updating those bibliographies. They are long—about 160 pages for Systematic Theology 1, 160 pages for ST2, 80 pages for ST3, and 120 pages for Ethics. Corresponding to some of those sources, I have prepared a zip folder for the students with hundreds of sources in PDF format. That is a helpful starting point for my students to research secondary sources.

[22] Email from Fred Zaspel to Andy Naselli, 12 July 2025 (shared with permission).

When you cite sources, the goal is not to prove to your audience that you did your homework. The goal is to investigate the evidence in order to establish what is true.

Tip 7. Organize your sources in Zotero.

The makers of Zotero describe it this way: "Zotero is a free, easy-to-use tool to help you collect, organize, annotate, cite, and share your research."[23] I use Zotero to store, manage, and cite resources—mainly books and articles. I have entered about 60,000 items into my Zotero library. Over half of them are PDFs. For my take on why and how to use Zotero, see my book *How to Read a Book*, "Appendix D: Why and How I Organize My Personal Library."[24]

For each item in Zotero, you can add notes to record quotations, summaries, and comments. When you are writing a research paper, you can create a temporary folder in which you place all the items you think are relevant for that paper. Then you can delete the items from that temporary folder as you work through them one by one. That's what I do when I write a book or article. If a footnote in the published version of one of my books mentions seven resources, then I most likely updated that footnote seven times along the way as I drafted the book. As I processed a book or article, I would update that footnote by adding that book or article to the footnote.

An old-school research method is to manually write down quotations, summaries, and comments on notecards and to develop a filing system for them.[25] That's how I learned to write papers in the 1990s. If you prefer that method and it is working well for you, that's fine. But I think using Zotero is more efficient and enjoyable.

---

[23] See https://www.zotero.org/. See also https://www.zotero.org/support/quick_start_guide.

[24] Naselli, *How to Read a Book*, 191–203.

[25] E.g., Nancy Jean Vyhmeister and Terry Dwain Robertson, *Your Guide to Writing Quality Research Papers: For Students of Religion and Theology*, 3rd ed. (Grand Rapids: Zondervan, 2014), 155–60.

(There are other electronic ways to organize your sources, but I prefer Zotero because I also use it to insert items in my footnotes and bibliography. Zotero is my hub for research.)

Tip 8. Take meticulous notes so that you accurately cite the source every time you quote, paraphrase, and summarize others.

If you fail to do this as you research, then you may unintentionally plagiarize. (See "Appendix A. Plagiarism: What is it, and how can you avoid it?")

Tip 9. Ask questions.

Be inquisitive. Ask lots of questions as you investigate. When you have a question that you don't know the answer to, write it down and see if you can discover the answer as you continue to explore your topic. Be curious.

Component 2. Organize the Paper:
Build a skeleton you can put flesh on.

Here are four tips.

Tip 1. Arrange your paper into a structured whole with three basic parts.[26]

Part 1: The Introduction. This need not be long. This is where you introduce the paper—perhaps in a way that creates interest by showing how important and relevant the topic is. At minimum, you should announce what the paper is about and how you organize what you argue. If you are proving a thesis (deductive), then you should state your thesis and how you attempt to prove it. If you are exploring a problem (inductive), then you should present the problem and how you attempt to examine it.

Part 2: The Body. This is the heart of your paper. This is where you make your case. You should arrange the main headings in a logical way. If you are arguing deductively, you may present a specific number of reasons that support your thesis. The reasons could be parallel or in order of importance. If you are arguing inductively, you may present evidence in an organized way (e.g., chronologically or thematically) that leads to a concluding thesis.

Part 3: The Conclusion. If you are arguing deductively, then restate the thesis. If you are arguing inductively, then state the thesis. Summarize your main arguments. You may choose to flesh out what your thesis implies or how it applies.[27]

---

[26] Cf. Brian J. Tabb, "What Makes a 'Good' Theological Article?," *Them* 49 (2024): 266–68.

[27] For more colorful writing, "The perfect ending should take your readers slightly by surprise and yet seem exactly right." William Zinsser, *On Writing Well: The Classic Guide to Writing Nonfiction*, 7th ed. (New York: Collins, 2006), 64. For example, in 2012, *Christianity Today* asked three people if churches should display the American flag in their sanctuaries: Douglas Wilson ("Just don't do it"), Lisa Velthouse ("It's all right by me"), and Russell D. Moore ("Fly it responsibly"). Wilson ends his short response with a zinger: "But being a Christian doesn't mean

Tip 2. Prepare a detailed outline of your paper early on in the process.

This will help you know where to add comments and arguments that come to mind as you research. Don't worry that drafting an outline will commit you to keeping that outline in the final version of your paper. This is a *provisional* outline, not a *permanent* one. You should keep tweaking the outline as you research and write.

Tip 3. State your main arguments clearly in headings.

Clear headings throughout a paper make it easier to follow your argument—like the headings I use in this little book. Clear headings makes the experience more pleasurable to read straight through the paper because you aren't wondering, "What exactly is the author trying to say here? I'm confused." Clear headings also make it easier to track the argument as you survey a paper to get the gist.

Tip 4. Use styles for the headings in your word processor.

For example, use Heading 1 for the top level, Heading 2 for the next, and Heading 3 for the next. This allows you to automatically create a table of contents and to navigate the paper on a screen via a document map. (If you are using a template that corresponds to the proper format, then the heading styles should be ready to go.)

---

we should hate our home country, just that we should know how to rightly order our allegiances. This is why, in my ideal scenario, the elders who vote in session to remove the American flag from the sanctuary should all have that same flag on their pickup trucks, right next to the gun rack." Douglas Wilson, Lisa Velthouse, and Russell D. Moore, "Should Churches Display the American Flag in Their Sanctuaries?," *Christianity Today* 56.7 (2012): 82.

Component 3. Develop a Coherent Argument:
Sharpen your reasoning, and avoid fallacies.

A coherent argument consists of a thesis, evidence, and analysis. Here are nine tips.

Tip 1. State your thesis clearly and concisely in a single sentence.

What if you can't state your thesis clearly and concisely in a single sentence? Then work harder to develop a coherent argument.

It may be helpful to state your thesis in one sentence and then clarify in the next sentence what you are *not* arguing. For example, "My thesis is that Christ's atonement is definite, not general. I am not arguing that there is no sense in which Jesus's atonement is universal. I am arguing that God intended for Jesus to die effectually for the sins of only the elect."

Tip 2. Don't overstate your thesis.

In your zeal to prove your thesis, be careful not to exaggerate. One way that students tend to express a thesis too strongly is to present it as if it is the theological or literary *theory of everything*—the secret key that unlocks the mysteries of the universe, the magic wand that unveils what no one has seen before, the thrilling discovery that will transform how you understand everything like never before. As you research, you may discover a truth that is new to you. That is exciting and rewarding, isn't it? But don't assume that you are the first one to discover that truth, and be careful not to overstate how important it is.

Tip 3. Support your thesis with sound reasons, and support your reasons with sufficient evidence.[28]

That is how you argue *persuasively*. A coherent argument logically progresses in a way that proves a thesis with reasons and evidence and analysis. A persuasive paper carefully examines the evidence and shows that it supports the thesis.

What counts as *sufficient* evidence? It depends on several factors:

- *The word limit*. A short essay can do only so much. A PhD dissertation should do much more. A research paper falls somewhere in between those two extremes.

- *The quality of the sources*. The sources you cite should be credible and authoritative. (On primary and secondary sources, see Component 1 above.)

- *The academic level*. Is this a paper for high school? College? Graduate school? For a more advanced level, the student should present more evidence and with more methodological rigor. That includes critically engaging the evidence as well as presenting and responding to counterarguments (see Component 4 below).

---

[28] According to *The Craft of Research*, a researcher should answer the following questions as he prepares to write a research paper:

1. What is my **claim**?
2. What **reasons** support my claim?
3. What **evidence** supports my reasons?
4. Do I **acknowledge** alternatives/complications/objections, and how do I **respond**?
5. What **principle** makes my reasons relevant to my claim? (We call this principle a **warrant**.)

Booth, Colomb, and Williams, *The Craft of Research*, 109 (bold emphasis in original).

Tip 4. Avoid fallacies.

A coherent argument avoids fallacies. And there are a lot of fallacies you could commit! I coauthored a book with D. A. Carson titled *Exegetical Fallacies*.[29] Yes, it's an entire book about fallacies you should avoid. (You're welcome!) Here's how we organize the fallacies:

- 17 word-study fallacies
- 7 grammatical fallacies (for NT Greek)
- 21 logical fallacies
- 5 presuppositional fallacies
- 5 literary fallacies
- 4 historical fallacies
- 5 theological fallacies

If you want help to avoid fallacies, then carefully read that book.

Tip 5. Answer the question "What would falsify my thesis?"

When I was a PhD student at Trinity Evangelical Divinity School, I observed a lot of dissertation proposals and dissertation defenses. The question that examiners most often asked students was this: "What would *falsify* your thesis?" In other words, what exactly would it take to *disprove* your thesis? It's an illuminating question because your answer may reveal that you are unaware of what might undermine your thesis. You may need to revise your thesis to make it more persuasive. You may need to support your thesis with additional arguments that respond to particular counterarguments.

For example, I believe that the Bible teaches that Jesus's atonement is definite, not general:

---

[29] D. A. Carson and Andrew David Naselli, *Exegetical Fallacies*, 3rd ed. (Grand Rapids: Baker Academic, 2026).

- *General* or *universal* atonement means that God intended for Jesus to die for the sins of all humans without exception.

- *Definite* or *limited* atonement means that God intended for Jesus to die effectually for the sins of only the elect.

What would falsify general atonement? Some proponents say that all it would take is a Bible passage that explicitly says that Jesus died *only* (key word) for the elect.

What would falsify definite atonement? I suggest that absolute negative language would falsify it.[30] Scripture distinctly emphasizes the universality of human sinfulness by using language that is more precise and is unequivocally unlimited. Mankind's sinfulness extends to all humans without exception. Perhaps the most effective way to communicate this through language is with absolute negatives, which are indisputably clear and unambiguously inclusive. For example, "Absalom has struck down *all* the king's sons; *not one* of them is left" (2 Sam 13:30 NIV).[31] Absolute negative language clarifies in order to avoid misunderstanding and emphasizes universality without exception. That is why when God wants to emphasize that every single human without exception is sinful, he expresses it with absolute negatives: "There is *no one* righteous, *not even one*.... There is *no one* who does good, *not even one*" (Rom 3:10, 12 NIV; cf. Ps 53:3). This language is unambiguous. God could use this type of language with reference to the extent of the atonement, but he does not. God has not stressed an unlimited nature of the extent of the atonement like he has the

---

[30] What follows is from Andrew David Naselli, "Conclusion," in *Perspectives on the Extent of the Atonement: 3 Views*, ed. Andrew David Naselli and Mark A. Snoeberger (Nashville: B&H Academic, 2015), 224–25.

[31] You can find scores of examples like this in the Bible by searching on the words "not one," "not even one," "no one," or "none." Cf. Exod 8:31; 9:6; 10:19; Num 1:19; Josh 10:8; 21:44; 23:14; Matt 24:2; Luke 12:6; John 17:12; 18:9; Acts 4:32; Rom 14:7.

doctrine of man's sinfulness. Scripture could say, "Christ died for *x* [e.g., *all humans* or *the whole world*]; there is *not one* human for whom Jesus did not die." That would falsify definite atonement.

Tip 6. Connect the seams of your arguments with smooth transitions.

Your arguments are the main substance of your paper. The icing on the cake is artfully connecting the seams of your arguments with smooth transitions. Skilled needlework creates seams that hold a patchwork quilt together, and smooth transition statements create seams that hold your arguments together. Transitions can securely stitch ideas together in an elegant way.

Transitions work differently in a research paper than they do for a speech. In a speech it is more important to include transitions that function like signposts. You are orally reminding your audience where you are in the argument. For example, in a sermon you may present and unpack four reasons from the Bible that Jesus is God. You may conclude each reason by restating it as you transition to the next reason: "So that's the third reason that Jesus is God: *The works Jesus did, is doing, and will do show that he is God.* Here's the fourth reason: *The worship Jesus receives shows that he is God.*" A transition like that is helpful when you are speaking, but it's unnecessary for a research paper. If you are presenting and unpacking four reasons in your paper, you may simply list each reason as a heading. You don't need to repeat each reason at the end of the section as you transition to the next reason.

However, it might be helpful to encourage the reader along with brief transitional statements that organically connect your arguments. There's not just one right way to include or exclude transitions. It's a judgment call. Transitions can be helpful if they make it easier to follow the argument. In a speech, you can use vocal cues like pauses and tone to guide the audience that you are shifting from one argument to another. In a paper, transitions can help compensate for lacking vocal cues.

Tip 7. Don't say what you feel; say what you think.

Your readers may not care about your feelings. When it comes to evaluating your *arguments*, how you feel is irrelevant to whether or not your arguments are strong. So don't say, "I feel …" when you argue. Instead, just argue.

Tip 8. Quote secondary sources strategically.

There are at least three good reasons to quote secondary sources in a research paper:

1. *Engage what others argue.* You can show how what you are arguing aligns with, differs from, or builds on what others have argued.

2. *Enhance what you argue.* Another author's specific wording may be so eloquent, pithy, or colorful that it's worth quoting rather than paraphrasing or just footnoting.

3. *Support what you argue.* For example, you may define *predestination* like this: God predetermined the destiny of certain individuals for salvation (i.e., *election* is choosing to save some) and others for condemnation (i.e., *reprobation* is choosing not to save others). Then to prove that this is the standard way that Reformed theologians define predestination, you could cite other theologians such as John Calvin, Francis Turretin, J. I. Packer, and Wayne Grudem.[32]

---

[32] This is what I do here: Andrew David Naselli, *Predestination: An Introduction*, Short Studies in Systematic Theology (Wheaton, IL: Crossway, 2024), 5–10.

Two warnings:

Don't quote too much. I can't give you a formula for when to quote and when not to quote. It's a wisdom call. A good rule of thumb is to quote sparingly.

Don't assume that quoting an authority proves your argument. D. A. Carson and I warn against this in *Exegetical Fallacies*:

> *Simplistic Appeal to Authority: To prove a conclusion by citing someone who agrees with it but without supporting the argument with reasons*
>
> This fallacy is thinking that appealing to an authority constitutes a reason for interpreting a text a certain way. The authority may be a distinguished scholar, a revered pastor, a cherished author, or simply the majority. Unless you give that authority's reasons for coming to that conclusion, such an appeal establishes only that you are under the influence of that particular authority or, at most, it lends the authority's general reputation in support of your position. But that is not a reasoned defense or explanation but merely an academic character reference.
>
> Doubtless we should be open to learning from all "authorities" in biblical and theological studies. But we should weigh what they say not on the basis of *who* said it but on the basis of the *reasons* they advance.[33]

Tip 9. Use an English dictionary and thesaurus as you write.

C. S. Lewis advises writers, "Be sure you know the meaning (or meanings) of every word you use."[34] To reason well, you need to speak precisely. To speak precisely, you need to use the right words. The humorist Mark Twain explains, "The difference between the *almost right* word and the *right* word is really a large matter—'tis

---

[33] Carson and Naselli, *Exegetical Fallacies*, 130.

[34] Lewis, *The Collected Letters of C. S. Lewis*, 3:1109.

the difference between the lightning bug and the lightning."[35] As Prov 25:11 says, "A word fitly spoken / is like apples of gold in a setting of silver." When you write a paper, your goal is to write clearly: "Say what you mean. Mean what you say. And let the glory of Christ shine through open statements of truth (2 Cor. 4:2)."[36]

To help you select fitting words, use an English dictionary and thesaurus as you write. On my MacBook, I use the Dictionary app, and I set it to display the *New Oxford American Dictionary* and the *Oxford American Writer's Thesaurus*. I use that app nearly every day. When I want to dig a little deeper, I consult two more dictionaries:

- Noah Webster's *American Dictionary of the English Language* (1st ed., 1828) is brilliantly clear and concise. (Bonus: Webster does not make up rebellious definitions for words like *man*, *woman*, and *marriage*. It can be helpful to see how English speakers used certain words prior to progressive influences.)

- The *Oxford English Dictionary* is the authority on what English words mean. There's a free version online and one that requires a subscription, which your library may subscribe to.[37] The paid version includes the history of each word across time. The entries note how definitions have changed, and they give specific examples for each definition.

---

[35] This is from Mark Twain's letter to George Bainton on October 15, 1888, first published in George Bainton, ed., *The Art of Authorship: Literary Reminiscences, Methods of Work, and Advice to Young Beginners* (New York: Appleton, 1890), 87–88.

[36] Jonathon Woodyard, "Clear as Christ: Why Direct Communication Is Vital for Christians," *Christ Over All*, 7 May 2025, https://christoverall.com/article/concise/clear-as-christ-why-direct-communication-is-vital-for-christians/.

[37] https://www.oed.com.

Component 4. Interact with Contrary Views:
Present and respond to the strongest opposing arguments.

A coherent argument consists of a thesis, evidence, and analysis. That analysis includes weighing *counterarguments*: "No argument is complete that fails to acknowledge and respond to other points of view."[38] As a general rule, a research paper that doesn't interact with any contrary views is a weak paper. When I encounter a thesis in a research paper I am grading, I think, "Who disagrees with this thesis? Why? Is the student aware of this? Will the student address that in this paper?"

Here are four tips.

Tip 1. Engage steel men, not straw men.

When you have formulated a strong thesis, you may be tempted to present and refute straw-man arguments. A straw-man argument distorts and weakens a position. It is easier to refute an argument if you present it in a weak form instead of its strongest form.

Instead, you should do the opposite. You should engage steel men, not straw men. In other words, you should present the strongest arguments against your view and then respond to those. If you do that well, then you will prove your thesis far more persuasively.

For example, don't refute Arminianism by citing some guy with a podcast or YouTube channel. If you're going to refute Arminianism, interact with the best arguments by the most articulate and informed Arminians.

Tip 2. Interact with specific statements.

Don't simply generically describe what Arminians believe or what Roman Catholicism teaches. Support what you assert by quoting an individual like the Arminian theologian Roger Olson, or quote a specific authoritative document like the Catechism of the

---

[38] Booth, Colomb, and Williams, *The Craft of Research*, 139.

Catholic Church. The best sources to interact with are influential and academically responsible.

Tip 3. Present and evaluate counterarguments fairly.

Here's a good diagnostic question to ask yourself: Would you critique an author differently if he were in the room listening to you evaluate him? Your goal when you present the view of an opponent is that he would say, "Yes, that's precisely my view. You are accurately representing me."

Tip 4. If you can't think of any contrary views to your thesis, then you should probably adjust your thesis.

I say *probably* because it's possible that you are arguing a thesis that others have not yet opposed in writing. But that would be exceptional. So as a general rule, your thesis should be controversial to some degree.[39] A non-controversial thesis is typically a non-starter for an academic research paper. For example, here are some non-controversial thesis statements:

- "Protestants believe that God exists." A more controversial thesis statement is "God exists." Many people have claimed that he doesn't.

- "Genesis 1:1 teaches that God created the heavens and the earth." A more controversial statement is "God created the heavens and the earth." Many people have rejected that God is the creator. Or "God created the heavens and the earth in the space of six 24-hour days."

---

[39] Paul describes a false teacher as having "an unhealthy craving for controversy and for quarrels about words" (1 Tim 6:4). A research paper should not have *that* kind of controversy. The problem that Paul is highlighting in 1 Tim 6:4 is not that a false teacher has a *healthy* curiosity about words. The problem is that a false teacher has a *sick* or *morbid* interest in silly quibbles about words. A false teacher wants to go to war against God's words.

Many Christians in the past few centuries have rejected young-earth creationism.

- "The Apostle Paul suffered." A more controversial statement is "God sovereignly ordains our suffering for his glory and our good." Many people think that a good God would never ordain our suffering.

Component 5. Write Clearly and Concisely:
Omit needless words.

I think this is the most memorable line from William Strunk's *The Elements of Style*: "Omit needless words." He explains,

> Vigorous writing is concise. A sentence should contain no unnecessary words, a paragraph no unnecessary sentences, for the same reason that a drawing should have no unnecessary lines and a machine no unnecessary parts. This requires not that the writer make all sentences short, or avoid all detail and treat subjects only in outline, but that every word tell.[40]

This section could be an entire book,[41] but I'll highlight just seven rules.

Rule 1. Use verbs instead of nominalizations (usually).[42]

Cannibals eat the flesh of fellow human beings, and words can eat fellow words. That's why Helen Sword refers to *nominalizations* as "zombie nouns."[43] You can create a nominalization by turning a word into a fancy-sounding noun:

- Implacable (an adjective) becomes *implacability.*
- Calibrate (a verb) becomes *calibration.*
- Crony (a noun) becomes *cronyism.*

---

[40] William Strunk Jr., *The Elements of Style*, ed. E. B. White, 4th ed. (Boston: Allyn and Bacon, 2000), 23. Cf. Michele T. Poff, ed., *The Elements of Style Workbook: Writing Strategies with Grammar Book* (Texas: Tip Top Education, 2017).

[41] E.g., Roy Peter Clark, *How to Write Short: Word Craft for Fast Times* (New York: Little, Brown, 2013).

[42] For rules 1 and 2, I'm updating Andrew David Naselli, "Zombie Nouns and Verbs: Why Nominalizations and Passives May Be Killing Your Writing," *Thoughts on Theology*, 3 February 2015, http://andynaselli.com/zombie-nouns-and-verbs-why-nominalizations-and-passives-may-be-killing-your-writing.

[43] Helen Sword, "Zombie Nouns," *New York Times*, 23 July 2012, http://opinionator.blogs.nytimes.com/2012/07/23/zombie-nouns/.

As a general rule, use verbs instead of the related nouns when possible. Which is clearer in the following table—the nominalizations or the verbs (see Fig. 5)?

Fig. 5. Nominalizations vs. Verbs

Nominalization	Verb
discovery	discover
discussion	discuss
failure	fail
fulfillment	fulfill
notification	notify
reaction	react
violation	violate
Helen Sword makes an *observation* that nominalizations decrease clarity [9 words].	Helen Sword *observes* that nominalizations decrease clarity [7 words].
Paul presents a *summary* of justification by faith [8 words].	Paul *summarizes* justification by faith [5 words].
John places an *emphasis* on faith [6 words].	John *emphasizes* faith [3 words].

A bonus is that when you use verbs instead of their related nouns, you use fewer words (see the final three rows of Fig. 5).

Using a nominalization may be the best option.[44] "In some cases nominalizations are useful, even necessary," Joseph Williams

---

[44] I use one in this very sentence—the word *nominalization* is a nominalization. I could avoid that by saying, "It may be the best option to nominalize a word." But in this context, that would be *less* clear.

qualifies,[45] but usually they muddy sentences and decrease clarity.[46] So as a general rule, avoid nominalizations since they often convolute and clutter instead of clarify.

Rule 2. Use the active voice instead of the passive voice (usually).

Which is clearer in the below table (Fig. 6)—passive or active?

Fig. 6. Passive vs. Active

Passive Voice	Active Voice
Mistakes were made.	I made mistakes.
It was done.	I did it.
Eli's sons were killed.	God killed Eli's sons.
The church building was stormed by protesters.	Protesters stormed the church building.
The ball was thrown.	John threw the ball.
The book was written in 1776.	Adam Smith wrote the book in 1776.
The decision was made to translate 1 Tim 2:12 as "to teach or to assume authority over a man."	The NIV Committee on Bible Translation decided to translate 1 Tim 2:12 as "to teach or to assume authority over a man."

---

[45] Joseph M. Williams, *Style: Toward Clarity and Grace*, Chicago Guides to Writing, Editing, and Publishing (Chicago: University of Chicago Press, 1990), 32.
[46] Cf. Steven Pinker, *The Sense of Style: The Thinking Person's Guide to Writing in the 21st Century* (New York: Viking, 2014), 50–52.

If you want to be clear and concise, use the active voice rather than the passive. This is a *general* rule. There are exceptions when the passive voice is better. For example, Paul's letter to the Galatians emphasizes that both Jews and Gentiles *are justified* (passive) by faith. I could say that God *justifies* (active) both Jews and Gentiles, but that doesn't quite capture what Paul says. Paul is not emphasizing that *God* justifies but that humans *are justified* in a certain way. I'm not sure how to capture that without using the passive.

Passives aren't always bad, but they should be the salt and pepper of a meal, not the steak. Students often overuse and misuse passives, and they are usually oblivious to it. They tend to use the passive voice mindlessly, not artfully. Skilled writers know how to use the passive voice well.[47]

Sometimes my students argue that passives are good since the NT is full of them. But the NT authors wrote in ancient Greek! I am arguing that we should communicate clearly in *modern-day English*. One of the ways to do that is to avoid passives as a general rule.

Rule 3. Don't try to sound smart.

John MacArthur remarked,

> It's very easy to be hard to understand. It only requires that you not know what you're talking about. And if you don't know what you're talking about, nobody else will either. It's very hard to be crystal-clear because in order to be crystal-clear you have to have mastered the text.[48]

---

[47] Cf. Pinker, *The Sense of Style*, 54–56.

[48] "John MacArthur 'Expository Leadership,'" interview by Austin T. Duncan, *The Master's Seminary*, 4 December 2012, https://www.youtube.com/watch?v=hFq9SBtvW0A&t=705s (see 11:45–12:45 min.).

Academic research papers are often boring and esoteric. Sadly, some academics work very hard to write that badly. They think it sounds smart. And some students try to imitate them.

It actually takes a lot more work to understand a challenging topic and then write about it in an *understandable* way. In other words, you have to work even harder to write about a complicated topic in a way that is both accurate and accessible. It takes a lot of skill to write about a complex topic in a way that non-experts can grasp.[49]

One of my graduate students came to my school's seminary program as a philosopher, and when I required him to summarize the theological message of Matthew's Gospel in one sentence, he wrote this: "The confluence of the ages is instantiated by the invasion of kingdom power and message, concomitants of newly arrived Messiah-King Jesus, the unifying telos and terminus of Old Testament hopes, types, and constructs." He meant this: "Jesus, who fulfills the OT, inaugurates the kingdom." I convinced him to change his writing style from what I call *academese* (or what another professor calls *jargonitis*[50]) to a style that normal English speakers can easily understand. (He took my challenge to heart, and he greatly improved.)

"Never say anything in writing that you wouldn't comfortably say in conversation."[51] The goal of writing a research paper is not to

---

[49] Cf. C. S. Lewis: "You must translate every bit of your Theology into the vernacular. This is very troublesome and it means you can say very little in half an hour, but it is essential. It is also of the greatest service to your own thought. I have come to the conviction that *if you cannot translate your thoughts into uneducated language, then your thoughts were confused.* Power to translate is the test of having really understood one's own meaning. A passage from some theological work for translation into the vernacular ought to be a compulsory paper in every Ordination examination." C. S. Lewis, "Christian Apologetics," in *God in the Dock: Essays on Theology and Ethics*, ed. Walter Hooper (Grand Rapids: Eerdmans, 1970), 98 (italics added).

[50] Helen Sword, *Stylish Academic Writing* (Cambridge: Harvard University Press, 2012), 112–21.

[51] Zinsser, *On Writing Well*, 26.

sound like a smart academic. So don't decorate your prose with fancy words and convoluted sentences that leave people thinking, "Huh? I don't know what he means, but he sure must be smart." Your paper should be readable.[52]

Rule 4. Be more specific than "points" or "things."

Speakers and writers often say something like this: "My sermon has three points," or "I'd like to share four things." Instead of saying that Paul "makes three points," say, "gives three reasons" or "shows three ways" or whatever. That is more specific and thus clearer. Wayne McDill lists 261 words that communicate more clearly than the ambiguous words *points* and *things*.[53]

Rule 5. It's OK to use first-person singular pronouns.

A more formal-sounding approach is to avoid ever saying "I" or "my" in a research paper. But sometimes the most natural and clear way to communicate is with a first-person singular pronoun. *The Chicago Manual of Style* advises, "When you need the first-person singular, use it. It is not immodest to use it; it is superstitious not to."[54]

---

[52] Cf. Kevin DeYoung: "Most students can't write well, because most scholars don't write well, because most people don't write well, because writing is really hard. It's one thing to read a lot and have a mastery of your material. It's another thing to present your material in clear, accessible—let alone arresting—prose. To be sure, there is plenty of writing that gets assigned to us for one reason or another. But I can almost guarantee it: the writers who actually *get* read, and the writers you actually *want* to read, are writers who write well. Don't settle for smart; work hard to communicate what you know in a way people can understand." Kevin DeYoung, "10 Lessons I've Learned While Working on My PhD," *Clearly Reformed*, 21 August 2018, https://clearlyreformed.org/10-lessons-ive-learned-working-phd/.

[53] I list them here: Andrew David Naselli, "Be More Specific Than 'Points' or 'Things,'" *Andy Naselli*, 8 May 2014, https://andynaselli.com/be-more-specific-than-points-or-things.

[54] *The Chicago Manual of Style*, 18th ed. (Chicago: The University of Chicago Press, 2024), §5.254 (p. 347).

Don't use the royal "we." Referring to yourself with "we" and "our" sounds pompous—as if you think you are royalty. It also feels overly formal to refer to yourself in the third person: "The author of this paper disagrees."

Rule 6. Close sheep gates.

C. S. Lewis explains that good writing is so clear that it closes sheep gates:

> The way for a person to develop a style is (a) to know exactly what he wants to say, and (b) to be sure he is saying exactly that. The reader, we must remember, does not start by knowing what we mean. If our words are ambiguous, our meaning will escape him. I sometimes think that writing is like driving sheep down a road. If there is any gate open to the left or the right the readers will most certainly go into it.[55]

> Always try to use the language so as to make quite clear what you mean and make sure [your] sentence couldn't mean anything else.[56]

> Take great pains to be *clear*. Remember that though you start by knowing what you mean, the reader doesn't, and a single ill-chosen word may lead him to a total misunderstanding.[57]

You aren't responsible for every time a reader misunderstands you. Sometimes the fault lies entirely with the reader. (How many times have people misunderstood God's words in the Bible? Those misunderstandings are not God's fault.) But as much as possible, anticipate reasonable misunderstandings, and clarify, "I mean *this*, not *that*."

---

[55] C.S. Lewis, "Cross-Examination," in *God in the Dock: Essays on Theology and Ethics*, ed. Walter Hooper (Grand Rapids: Eerdmans, 1970), 291.
[56] Lewis, *The Collected Letters of C. S. Lewis*, 3:766.
[57] Lewis, *The Collected Letters of C. S. Lewis*, 3:1108 (italics in original).

Rule 7. Use a table if it helps organize information clearly.

I love a good table. If a picture is worth a thousand words, then a good table is worth a thousand sentences (OK, maybe not a thousand—but a lot).

I include tables in this book because I think they help organize information clearly. A good table concisely compares, summarizes, and clarifies ideas. It can make complex ideas more accessible, reduce the word count, and make a text-heavy paper more readable.

A good table is simple in that you can look at it and immediately understand what it is doing. It should have a clear title, clear headings, and no clutter.

Component 6. Use Proper Grammar, Syntax, and Format: Remove distractions by mastering the mechanics.

It is extremely unpleasant to read a paper that is full of improper grammar, syntax, and format. The difference between reading a paper *with* such errors versus a paper *without* them is like the difference between driving on a jarringly rutted and potholed road versus a newly paved road. When a professor is reading a student's research paper, he wants to focus on the content and the argument, but it's hard to think about that if the grammar and style are a mess. So *remove distractions by mastering the mechanics.*

Here are twenty-four rules.

Rule 1. Use a template (if one is available).

A template is a preset format for a text document that you can use so you don't have to recreate the format each time you write a research paper. If such a template is available, use it.

- You shouldn't use the wrong font or font size.

- You shouldn't omit the title on the top of page 1.

- You shouldn't use the wrong styles for headings or the body or footnotes or the bibliography or quotations.

- You shouldn't mess up the title page or page numbering.

- You shouldn't use orphan headings. An *orphan heading* is a heading that occurs at the bottom of a page all by itself with no text following it on that page. Instead, the text begins on the first line of the next page. You should use styles for your headings that automatically "Keep with Next" to make it impossible for an orphan heading to occur.

Use a template.

Rule 2. Cite sources in footnotes and the bibliography correctly.

What is the correct format? Follow the format your professor requires. My students must follow *The SBL Handbook of Style* (2nd ed.).[58] Here are eight citation issues to beware.

Citation Issue 1. Cite the names and places of presses correctly.

Chapter 6 in *The SBL Handbook of Style* ("Notes and Bibliographies," pp. 68–108) includes a section on names and places of presses (pp. 76–82). Here are some examples:

- Wrong: Wheaton: Crossway Publishers, 2016.
- Right: Wheaton, IL: Crossway, 2016.

- Wrong: Grand Rapids, MI: Zondervan Books.
- Right: Grand Rapids: Zondervan.

Citation Issue 2. Use the author's published name.

If a book's title page lists the author as D. A. Carson, then don't write Donald A. Carson or Don Carson.

---

[58] *The SBL Handbook of Style: For Biblical Studies and Related Disciplines*, 2nd ed. (Atlanta: SBL Press, 2014). See also the "Student Supplement for *The SBL Handbook of Style*, Second Edition," https://www.sbl-site.org/wp-content/uploads/2025/04/SBLHSsupp2015-02.pdf. Cf. Andrew David Naselli, review of *The SBL Handbook of Style: For Biblical Studies and Related Disciplines*, 2nd ed., *Them* 40 (2015): 95–97, https://andynaselli.com/wp-content/uploads/2015_SBLHS_review.pdf. See also "Citing URLs," *SBL Handbook of Style: Explanations, Clarifications, and Expansions*, 1 June 2016, https://sblhs2.com/2016/06/01/citing-urls/. My students follow the most recent version of *The Chicago Manual of Style* as a backup for anything the *SBL Handbook* doesn't address.

Citation Issue 3. Don't mix up the author(s) and the editor(s).

Sometimes students mistakenly cite an article in an edited book by the name of the editor(s) instead of the author(s) who wrote that article.

Citation Issue 4. Cite actual page numbers if a book is available in print.

Don't cite Kindle locations for a book if there is a print version.

Citation Issue 5. Enter the bibliographic information for an item into Zotero precisely.

One of my above tips is "Organize your resources in Zotero." If you use Zotero, then it is crucial that you enter the bibliographic information for a book or article into Zotero perfectly. If you do, then you can automatically insert the bibliographic information for an item into your paper's footnotes and bibliography with impeccable SBL format (or whatever format your professor requires). If any of the information is incorrect in Zotero, then it will be incorrect in your paper as well.

Citation Issue 6. Use short titles for subsequent references.

The first time you footnote a resource, include full bibliographic information. The rest of the times you cite that same resource, cite only the author's last name plus a shortened version of the title. Here are two examples:

- First reference: Andrew David Naselli, *Predestination: An Introduction*, Short Studies in Systematic Theology (Wheaton, IL: Crossway, 2024), 143–49.
- Subsequent references: Naselli, *Predestination*, 148.

- First reference: Peter J. Gentry and Stephen J. Wellum, *Kingdom through Covenant: A Biblical-Theological Understanding of the Covenants*, 2nd ed. (Wheaton, IL: Crossway, 2018), 51–105.
- Subsequent references: Gentry and Wellum, *Kingdom through Covenant*, 673.

You don't need to worry about this if you use Zotero. When you enter bibliographic information for an item in Zotero, simply enter the "Short Title."

Citation Issue 7. Don't include standard reference works in your bibliography.

For example, if you cite BDAG[59] or English Bible translations in a seminary paper, there's no need to list them in your bibliography. An exception to this rule is if the topic of your paper is a standard reference work (e.g., a research paper on the ESV).

Citation Issue 8. In book titles that have & (the ampersand symbol), spell it out as "and," but for publisher names that have &, leave the ampersand symbol.

If the book cover says, *Snakes & Dragons*, then cite that book as *Snakes and Dragons*. If the publisher is Vandenhoeck & Ruprecht, then cite it that way (not as "Vandenhoeck and Ruprecht").

***Rule 3. Stay within the word count.*[60]**

Don't go above or below the word count by a single word. If the range is 3,500–5,000 words, don't write 3,499 words or 5,001 words.

---

[59] Walter Bauer, Frederick William Danker, William F. Arndt, and F. Wilbur Gingrich, eds., *A Greek-English Lexicon of the New Testament and Other Early Christian Literature*, 3rd ed. (Chicago: University of Chicago Press, 2000).
[60] Professors, I encourage you to give students a word count (e.g., 3,500–5,000 words) instead of a page count (e.g., 12–15 pages). The reason is that there are

This takes discipline, and it's good training for you as a writer and communicator. It shows a lack of discipline if your paper is above or below the word count. If the paper you drafted is over the word count and you don't want to lose any of your work, then save the excess in another document, or move it to an appendix in your paper (and don't expect your professor to read appendices).

Rule 4. Use the hyphen (-), en dash (–), and em dash (—) correctly.[61]

Fig. 7. How to Use a Hyphen, En Dash, and Em Dash

	Use	Correct	Incorrect
hyphen (-)	Connect compound words and joint modifiers (but not -ly adverbs).	• one-third • half-baked idea • spiritually dead man	• one third • half baked idea • spiritually-dead man
en dash (–)	Indicate a range (e.g., references, pages, dates).	• Rom 1:16–17 • pages 113–14 • 1980–2025	• Rom 1:16-17 • pages 113-14 • 1980-2025

---

tricks to pack way more words into a particular page count (e.g., moving content to footnotes or tweaking the margins, line spacing, character spacing, and/or font).
[61] Cf. "Hyphens, En Dashes, Em Dashes," *The Chicago Manual of Style Online*, https://www.chicagomanualofstyle.org/qanda/data/faq/topics/HyphensEnDashesEmDashes/faq0002.html; "Hyphens, En Dashes, and Em Dashes," *SBL Handbook of Style: Explanations, Clarifications, and Expansions*, 1 November 2016, https://sblhs2.com/2016/11/01/hyphens-en-dashes-em-dashes/.

	Use	Correct	Incorrect
em dash (—)	Indicate an aside, emphasis, or interruption.	• "Do you suppose, O man—you who judge those who practice such things and yet do them yourself—that you will escape the judgment of God?" (Rom 2:3). • Shakespeare's *Macbeth*—a tragedy of ambition—explores human depravity.	

Tip: Learn shortcuts on your computer's keyboard for the en dash and em dash:

- Shortcuts for Mac:
  - en dash = option + - or --
  - em dash = option + shift + - or ---

- Shortcuts for Windows:
  - en dash = alt + 0150
  - em dash = alt + 0151

Rule 5. Punctuate correctly.

Here are nineteen common issues. (There are many others.[62])

Fig. 8. Common Punctuation Issues

Rule	Correct	Incorrect
1. Add a comma before a coordinating conjunction (and, but, or, nor, for, yet) that joins two independent clauses.	• I appreciate Shakespeare, but I enjoy C. S. Lewis more. • I appreciate Shakespeare but enjoy C. S. Lewis more.	• I appreciate Shakespeare but I enjoy C. S. Lewis more. • I appreciate Shakespeare, but enjoy C. S. Lewis more.

---

[62] To better understand the English language, see Bryan A. Garner, *The Chicago Guide to Grammar, Usage, and Punctuation, Chicago Guides to Writing, Editing, and Publishing* (Chicago: University of Chicago Press, 2016); Bryan A. Garner, *Garner's Modern English Usage*, 5th ed. (Oxford: Oxford University Press, 2022). Garner is an authority on English grammar and style. He wrote the "Grammar and Usage" chapter for *The Chicago Manual of Style*.

Rule	Correct	Incorrect
2. Use the Oxford comma (i.e., the comma before the final item in a list).	• The potluck featured dishes from Pastor Jack, a pastor, and a heretic. • The book discusses the suffering of Hannah, Samuel, and Boaz's wife. • The father told a story about his children, a clown, and a magician.	• The potluck featured dishes from Pastor Jack, a pastor and a heretic. (Watch out for Pastor Jack!) • The book discusses the suffering of Hannah, Samuel and Boaz's wife. (Hannah has two husbands?) • The father told a story about his children, a clown and a magician. (Two interesting children!)
3. Don't place footnote numbers *before* a comma, semicolon, period, or quotation mark.	• I agree with Calvin,[10] • I agree with Calvin;[10] • I agree with Calvin.[10] • "I agree with Calvin."[10]	• I agree with Calvin[10], • I agree with Calvin[10]; • I agree with Calvin[10]. • "I agree with Calvin.[10]"
4. Add quotation marks *after* a period or comma.	• I answered, "Chipotle."	• I answered, "Chipotle".

Rule	Correct	Incorrect
5. Add commas around nonrestrictive or nonessential clauses. (See also Rule 20 below: "Don't confuse 'which' and 'that.'")	• The apostle Paul, *who wrote thirteen NT letters*, was prolific.	• The apostle Paul *who wrote thirteen NT letters* was prolific. (As opposed to another apostle Paul who wrote a different number of NT letters?)
	• He loves his wife, *who is a faithful woman.*	• He loves his wife *who is a faithful woman.* (As opposed to his wives who aren't faithful?)
	• That book belongs to my firstborn child, *who loves to read Shakespeare.*	• That book belongs to my firstborn child *who loves to read Shakespeare.* (As opposed to my other firstborn children?)
6. Do not add commas around restrictive or essential clauses.	• The author *who wrote Romans* was prolific. • My daughter *who recently graduated from high school* is a student at Bethlehem College.	• The author, *who wrote Romans*, was prolific. • My daughter, *who recently graduated from high school*, is a student at Bethlehem College. (I have four daughters.)

Rule	Correct	Incorrect
7. Add a comma after the abbreviations "e.g." (for example) and "i.e." (that is) but not for "cf." (confer or compare).	<ul><li>(e.g., see Calvin's *Institutes*)</li><li>(i.e., Calvin's *Institutes*)</li><li>(cf. Calvin's *Institutes*)</li></ul>	<ul><li>(e.g. see Calvin's *Institutes*)</li><li>(i.e. Calvin's *Institutes*)</li><li>(cf., Calvin's *Institutes*)</li></ul>
8. Don't put "ff." after a verse reference. Specify the precise range.	<ul><li>Rom 3:21–26</li></ul>	<ul><li>Rom 3:21ff.</li></ul>
9. Form the possessive for all names with an apostrophe *s* (including for Jesus and Moses).	<ul><li>Jesus's</li><li>Moses's</li></ul>	<ul><li>Jesus'</li><li>Moses'</li></ul>
10. If you isolate a Greek word or phrase and if the single word or the final Greek word in a phrase has a grave accent in its context, change the grave accent to an acute accent.	<ul><li>γάρ</li><li>εἰ ὁ θεός</li></ul>	<ul><li>γὰρ</li><li>εἰ ὁ θεὸς</li></ul>
11. Don't place quotation marks around Hebrew or Greek words.	<ul><li>the phrase ἐν ταῖς ἐσχάταις ἡμέραις</li></ul>	<ul><li>the phrase "ἐν ταῖς ἐσχάταις ἡμέραις"</li></ul>

Rule	Correct	Incorrect
12. Use only one space between sentences. (The two-space rule accommodated manual typewriters with monospaced type.)	• There is only one space after this sentence. This is the way.	• There are two spaces after this sentence. This is not the way.
13. Separate Scripture references with a semicolon, not a comma (unless you are separating verse references in the same chapter).	• Acts 20:32; 26:18; 1 Cor 1:2; 6:11; Heb 10:10, 14	• Acts 20:32, 26:18, 1 Cor 1:2, 6:11, Heb 10:10, 14
14. Use single and double quotation marks correctly when you punctuate a quotation within a quotation.[63]	• Lloyd-Jones explains, "Man according to this view, and in spite of the phrase 'let go and let God,' seems to play the most vital part in the process."	• Lloyd-Jones explains, "Man according to this view, and in spite of the phrase "let go and let God," seems to play the most vital part in the process."

---

[63] British punctuation works differently. (I've asked some of my academic British friends to explain it to me, and they concede that British punctuation is inconsistent and not as standardized as American English.) If you are quoting a British publication as a block quote, do not update the punctuation to American English; keep it as it appears in the original.

Rule	Correct	Incorrect
15. Don't introduce a direct quotation with "that." Use "that" to introduce indirect quotations.	• DeYoung asserts, "We cannot see God without seeing all three persons at the same time." • DeYoung asserts that we cannot see the one true God without simultaneously seeing all three persons.	• DeYoung asserts that "we cannot see God without seeing all three persons at the same time."
16. Don't place quotation marks around a block quote.	Pretend that this is a long block quote.	"Pretend that this is a long block quote."

65

Rule	Correct	Incorrect
17. Use colons properly. • The clause before a colon must be a complete sentence (i.e., an independent clause). • A colon may introduce an explanation, list, elaboration, question, or quotation. • Don't capitalize the first word after the colon unless it is a proper noun or it starts a complete sentence.	• The first question is this: What is sanctification? • Bavinck puts it starkly: "A predominantly choleric or phlegmatic woman is unpleasantly masculine; a sanguine or melancholic man is unpleasantly feminine." • These are his favorite theologians: Augustine, Calvin, Luther, Edwards, and Bavinck. • Systematic theologies typically portray a Christian's salvation with three tenses: past (justification), present (sanctification), and future (glorification).	• The first question is: what is sanctification? • Bavinck puts it starkly, "A predominantly choleric or phlegmatic woman is unpleasantly masculine; a sanguine or melancholic man is unpleasantly feminine." • His favorite theologians are: Augustine, Calvin, Luther, Edwards, and Bavinck. • Systematic theologies typically portray a Christian's salvation with three tenses, past (justification), present (sanctification), and future (glorification).

Rule	Correct	Incorrect
18. Use semicolons properly. A semicolon may *connect* independent clauses or *separate* items: • A semicolon may connect closely related independent clauses (i.e., complete sentences). Such a connection is weaker than a conjunction like *and* or *but*, and it is stronger than a period. • A semicolon may separate items in a complex list to ensure clarity.	• Higher life theology has two steps: first you get saved; then you get serious. • The book discusses the theology of Jonathan Edwards, a pastor and theologian; C. S. Lewis, a literary scholar; and D. A. Carson, a NT scholar.	• This paper addresses a single topic; predestination. (Use a colon instead.) • His favorite theologians are Augustine; Calvin; Luther; Edwards; and Bavinck. (Use commas instead.)

Rule	Correct	Incorrect
19. Use an ellipsis properly.[64] An ellipsis (a series of three dots) indicates omitted material in a quotation. You must preserve the original meaning without altering what the author intended to communicate through his words. • *Within a sentence:* Place a space before and after the ellipsis. • *At the end of a sentence:* Use four dots (a period + three ellipsis dots). Place the period immediately after the final word with no space before the ellipsis.	• "God's providence … is perfect." • "An overseer must be above reproach…. He must manage his own household well" (1 Tim 3:2, 4).	• "God's providence…is perfect." (Add a space before and after the ellipsis.) • "An overseer must be above reproach …. He must manage his own household well" (1 Tim 3:2, 4). (Delete the space before the ellipsis.) • John Piper says, "I … agree with everything Andy Naselli says." (That's misleading.[65])

Rule 6. Capitalize theological words correctly.

For theological words, follow *The SBL Handbook of Style* (pp. 37–52). For example,

---

[64] Cf. *SBL Handbook of Style*, §4.1.3 (pp. 15–16); *Chicago Manual of Style*, §12.59–69 (pp. 760–65).

[65] "Noel and I saw *Courageous* and agree with everything Andy Naselli says about it." John Piper, post on X, 6 September 2011, https://x.com/JohnPiper/status/111159254374813696.

- biblical (not Biblical)
- covenant (not Covenant)
- Gospel (not gospel) when it refers to the Gospel of Matthew, Mark, Luke, or John
- gospel (not Gospel) when it refers to good news
- kingdom of God (not Kingdom of God)
- Messiah (not messiah)
- messianic (not Messianic)
- temple (not Temple)

Don't capitalize pronouns referring to deity.[66] Some people prefer that practice to indicate that a "you" or "he" or "him" refers to God and not to someone else, and some prefer it to signal respect for God. I respect those reasons, but I don't capitalize pronouns for deity because it is unnecessary and can create theological problems. What do you do with a psalm of David that is Messianic? Do you capitalize the pronouns and titles for David if David is a type of Christ? Today nearly all Christian publishers and English Bible translations don't capitalize pronouns for deity, and that was also the case for the earliest English Bible translations, such as the King James Version.

Rule 7. Use title case correctly.

The headings of your research paper should use *title case*. (*The Chicago Manual of Style* used to call this form of capitalization *headline style*. Now it uses the label *title case* as opposed to *sentence case*.) Follow the *Chicago Manual of Style*:[67]

---

[66] Cf. Mark Ward, "Why We Should Not Capitalize Deity Pronouns When Referring to God," *Word by Word*, 8 June 2017, https://www.logos.com/grow/why-we-should-not-capitalize-deity-pronouns-when-referring-to-god/.

[67] *Chicago Manual of Style*, §8.160–61 (pp. 569–70).

1. Capitalize the first and last words in titles and subtitles …
   and all other major words (nouns, pronouns, verbs,
   adjectives, adverbs, and some conjunctions—but see rule
   4).
2. Lowercase the articles *the*, *a*, and *an*.
3. Lowercase prepositions of fewer than five letters, except
   when they are used adverbially or or adjectivally (*up* in
   Look Up, *down* in *Turn Down*, *on* in *The On Button*, *to* in
   Come To, etc.) or when they compose part of a Latin
   expression used adjectivally or adverbially (*De Facto*, *In
   Vitro*, etc.). In cases, a shorter preposition may be
   capitalized when paired with a longer preposition (*for* in
   For and Against). Note that the five-letter rule includes
   abbreviations (e.g., *Versus* would be capitalized, but *vs.*
   would not be).
4. Lowercase the common coordinating conjunctions *and*,
   but, *for*, *or*, and *nor*.
5. Lowercase *to* not only as a preposition (rule 3) but also as
   part of an infinitive (*to Run*, *to Hide*, etc.) and lowercase
   as in any grammatical function.
6. Lowercase the part of a proper name that would be
   lowercase in text, such as *de* or *von*.

… Examples of title case [with the corresponding rules in
parentheses] …

Mnemonics That Work Are Better Than Rules That Do Not
Singing While You Work
A Little Learning Is a Dangerous Thing (2)
Four Theories Concerning the Gospel According to Matthew
(2, 3)
"The Trouble with Tribbles": Much Ado About Nothing? (3)
The Case For and Against AI (3)
Writing Under a Deadline and Without an Editor (2, 3, 4)
Taking Down Names, Spelling Them Out, and Typing Them
Up (3, 4)
Tired but Happy (4)
The Editor as Anonymous Assistant (5) …

Defenders of da Vinci Fail the Test: The Name Is Leonardo (2, 3, 6)

Sitting on the Floor in an Empty Room (2, 3), *but* Turn On, Tune In, and Enjoy (3, 4)

Ten Hectares per Capita, *but* Landownership and Per Capita Income (3)

Progress in In Vitro Fertilization (3)

The most common word I notice students capitalize incorrectly is the word *is*. In title case, it should be *Is* (not *is*):

- right: *All That Is in God*
- wrong: *All That is in God*

If you are not sure if you are capitalizing a title correctly, you can double-check by entering it at the "Capitalize My Title" website (use the "Chicago" style).[68]

Rule 8. Abbreviate correctly.

Follow chapter 8 in *The SBL Handbook of Style* (pp. 117–260), especially for books of the Bible (pp. 124–25). For example,

- Gen 3:16 (not Gen. 3:16 or Genesis 3:16)
- Rom 3 (not Rom. 3 or Romans 3)

Two exceptions: Spell out the book name if (1) a chapter (or chapter and verse) does not follow it or (2) it comes first in the sentence. For example,

- right: Paul wrote Romans in about AD 57.
- wrong: Paul wrote Rom in about AD 57.

---

[68] https://capitalizemytitle.com/style/Chicago/.

- right: Romans 3:21–26 is the most important paragraph in the Bible.
- wrong: Rom 3:21–26 is the most important paragraph in the Bible.

- right: First Corinthians 13 is about love.
- wrong: 1 Cor 13 is about love.

- right: The NT frequently quotes Ps 110.
- wrong: The New Testament frequently quotes Psalm 110.

Rule 9. Footnote what translation you are using the first time you quote Scripture.

Say something like this: "Scripture quotations are from the ESV." Or "Scripture quotations are from the ESV unless otherwise noted."[69]

Also, as a general rule, use a standard translation. In my first PhD seminar with D. A. Carson at Trinity Evangelical Divinity School, a student was defending his paper in front of the class, and Dr. Carson asked him something like this: "Why do you use your own rigidly form-based translation in your paper? That is a very MDiv-ish thing to do. Why not simply use one of the standard translations like the NIV or ESV and then diverge from that when you think that would be helpful?"

Rule 10. Minimize saying "chapter" and "verse" when you refer to Bible passages.

Chapter divisions go back only to the 1200s, and Bible verses didn't exist until about 1550. Chapters and verses are helpful for locating specific sentences and phrases efficiently, but that's about it. Instead of referring to chapters and verses in the Bible, it's better (as

---

[69] I know—the sentence has both a nominalization ("quotations") and a passive ("noted"). It's legit rule-breaking.

much as possible) to refer to the Bible as *literature*. Use *literary* terms like section, paragraph, sentence, command, phrase, proverb, stanza, parable, and story.[70]

- Avoid: Verse 12 says, "Fight the good fight of the faith."
- Better: Paul commands, "Fight the good fight of the faith" (1 Tim 6:12).

Rule 11. Cite Scripture references in the body rather than the footnotes (usually).

Here are some examples:

- God has created both male and female in his image (Gen 1:27; 9:6; Jas 3:9).
- The apostles testified that God raised Christ (e.g., Acts 2:24), but that is false if God does not resurrect the bodies of dead people (1 Cor 15:13, 16).
- Paul portrays the Christian life as walking (Rom 6:4; 8:4; 2 Cor 5:7; Gal 5:16; Eph 5:2; Col 1:10).
- Paul portrays the Christian life as warfare (2 Cor 10:3–5; Eph 6:10–18; 1 Tim 1:18; 6:12; 2 Tim 2:3; 4:7).

---

[70] I appreciate what Gordon Fee writes in the preface to the second edition of his commentary on 1 Corinthians: "A ... change from the first edition is related to another passion engendered from many years of teaching, writing, and listening to sermons—namely, to eliminate the language of 'chapter and verse,' a system of numbers absolutely essential for 'finding things' but otherwise totally foreign to the first-century author. Paul wrote words put into sentences, which in the present written culture also require paragraphs. But he did not write 'verses,' language that has inherently, but not purposefully, created a misguided use of Scripture that would be foreign to the original authors. So I have tried to relegate the numbers to parentheses, rather than use such language in the text of the commentary itself. This in itself required a third and final reading of the text in an attempt to be faithful to Paul, while still trying to help the reader 'find things' regarding the rest of the biblical revelation." Gordon D. Fee, *The First Epistle to the Corinthians*, 2nd ed., NICNT (Grand Rapids: Eerdmans, 2014), xvii.

It's better to put those Scripture references in parentheses than in a footnote. The exception is that it may be prudent to use a footnote if the list of references is particularly long (e.g., two full lines).

Rule 12. Format poetry as poetry, not as prose.

About 30–40% of the Bible is poetry. The very form of the literature communicates the meaning with parallelism and other poetic structures. Poetry is different from prose, which includes narrative, epistles, legal texts, and genealogies.

When you quote poetry, don't format it as prose:

> Blessed is the man who walks not in the counsel of the wicked, nor stands in the way of sinners, nor sits in the seat of scoffers; but his delight is in the law of the LORD, and on his law he meditates day and night. (Ps 1:1–2)

When you quote poetry, format it as poetry:

> Blessed is the man
>   who walks not in the counsel of the wicked,
> nor stands in the way of sinners,
>   nor sits in the seat of scoffers;
> but his delight is in the law of the LORD,
>   and on his law he meditates day and night. (Ps 1:1–2)

If you want to conserve space, then add line breaks:

> Blessed is the man / who walks not in the counsel of the wicked, / nor stands in the way of sinners, / nor sits in the seat of scoffers; / but his delight is in the law of the LORD, / and on his law he meditates day and night. (Ps 1:1–2)

Rule 13. Avoid misplaced modifiers.

In my experience the modifier that students most often misplace is the word *only*. Place the word *only* immediately before the word or phrase it modifies.

This is correct: "The weak person eats *only* vegetables" (Rom 14:2). The word *only* modifies *vegetables*. The meaning of the sentence changes if you move the word *only* around:

- *Only* the weak person eats vegetables. (A strong person does not eat vegetables.)

- The *only* weak person eats vegetables. (There is only one weak person.)

- The weak person *only* eats vegetables. (He doesn't do anything else with vegetables: he doesn't grow them, buy them, sell them, drink them, carry them, etc.)

Or try moving the word *only* immediately before each word in the following sentence: "I hit him in the eye yesterday."[71] The meaning changes each time. (The same rule applies for similar words like *primarily*.)

Another common misplaced modifier is an entire phrase:

- wrong: *Laid out over a charcoal fire*, Jesus offered fish to his disciples. (Jesus was not laid out over the charcoal fire. The fish were.)
- better: Jesus offered to his disciples fish *that he had laid out over a charcoal fire*.

I still remember sitting in a college class when Dr. Layton Talbert illustrated dangling modifiers like this: "Sizzling juicily on the grill, Bob could hardly wait to eat those hamburgers." He told the class, "If you mean that the hamburgers are sizzling juicily on the grill, keep poor Bob off the hibachi!"

---

[71] "Usage of the Word *Only*," *SBL Handbook of Style: Explanations, Clarifications, and Expansions*, 15 March 2018, https://sblhs2.com/2018/03/15/usage-of-the-word-only/.

Beware dangling participles: "*Sweating in the hot and humid garage*, the fan felt refreshing to Dustin." No, the fan wasn't sweating; Dustin was. A dangling participle grammatically modifies the wrong noun.

Rule 14. Don't assert that something is "clear"; show that it's clear.

C. S. Lewis teaches that good writing *shows* you more than it *tells* you:

> Never use adjectives or adverbs which are mere appeals to the reader to feel as you want him to feel. He won't do it just because you ask him: you've got to *make* him. No good *telling* us a battle was 'exciting'. If *you* succeeded in exciting us the adjective will be unnecessary: if you don't, it will be useless. Don't tell us the jewels had an 'emotional' glitter; make us feel the emotion. I can hardly tell you how important this is.[72]

> Don't use adjectives which merely tell us how you want us to *feel* about the thing you are describing. I mean, instead of telling us a thing was 'terrible', describe it so that we'll be terrified. Don't say it was 'delightful': make *us* say 'delightful' when we've read the description. You see, all those words, (horrifying, wonderful, hideous, exquisite) are only like saying to your readers 'Please will you do my job for me.'[73]

The main way that advice applies to a research paper is to avoid asserting that a contested idea is *clear*. It's better to *show* that it's clear.

---

[72] Lewis, *The Collected Letters of C. S. Lewis*, 3:881 (italics original).
[73] Lewis, *The Collected Letters of C. S. Lewis*, 3:766 (italics original).

Rule 15. Avoid "let us" or "we see."

"Let us" typically begins a sentence in which you exhort someone else to do something. For example, Paul exhorts, "*Let us* cast off the works of darkness and put on the armor of light. *Let us* walk properly as in the daytime" (Rom 13:12b–13a). That is a fitting way to communicate in a sermon, but as a general rule it is not fitting for a research paper (except perhaps sometimes in a paper's conclusion). A research paper is not a sermon.

Another phrase to avoid is "we see." It's better simply to say what you mean:

- avoid: "We see in John 1:1 that Jesus is God."
- better: "John 1:1 teaches that Jesus is God."

Rule 16. Emphasize using italics.

If you want to emphasize a word or words, don't use **bold** or ALL CAPS or *asterisks*. Use *italics*.

As a general rule, it's also better to use italics instead of quotation marks when you are singling out a word:

- avoid: The word "monergism" means …
- better: The word *monergism* means …

Rule 17. Don't indicate that a book is the first edition.

Indicate when a book is a second or later edition, but there's no need to indicate that it is the first edition. We assume that a book is the first edition unless you specify otherwise.

An exception is if you are intentionally distinguishing the first edition from later editions. For example, you may be comparing different editions of Calvin's *Institutes*. When I share the tip "Use an English dictionary and thesaurus as you write" (under Component 3 above), I say that I use Noah Webster's *American Dictionary of the English Language* (1st ed., 1828). I specify the first edition to distinguish it from the many subsequent editions.

Rule 18. Don't misspell words.

There's no excuse for this with spell checkers. Be careful not to confuse homophones like *there* and *their* or *its* and *it's*.

Rule 19. Specify how an adverbial participle modifies a verb.[74]

Don't leave the relation between a main verb and an adverbial participle ambiguous. Clarify how the participle modifies the verb. You can figure out how they relate by stating the main verb and then the participle (with an *-ing*). For example, in the sentence "Christ emptied himself, taking the form of a servant," the main verb is *emptied*, and the adverbial participle is *taking*. So you want to figure out how *taking* modifies *emptied*: "Christ *emptied* himself *taking*." (See the first example in Fig. 9 below.)

Fig. 9. Ways to Clarify an Ambiguous Adverbial Participle

Ambiguous	Clear	Label and Definition
Christ emptied himself, *taking* the form of a servant.	Christ emptied himself *by taking* the form of a servant.	Means: The participle expresses the *means* by which the verb's action occurs.
The woman came and fell down before him, *having become frightened and trembling*.	The woman came and fell down before him *in a frightened and trembling manner*.	Manner: The participle expresses the *manner* in which the verb's action occurs.
No one *lighting* a lamp puts it in a cellar.	No one *after lighting* a lamp puts it in a cellar.	Time: The participle expresses *when* the verb's action occurs.

---

[74] I am condensing Naselli, *How to Understand and Apply the New Testament*, 103–7. (A second edition of this book is forthcoming in 2027.)

Ambiguous	Clear	Label and Definition
Be steadfast, immovable, abounding in the work of the Lord always, *knowing* that your labor is not in vain in the Lord.	Be steadfast, immovable, abounding in the work of the Lord always *because you know* that your labor is not in vain in the Lord.	Cause: The participle expresses a *cause* or *ground* for the verb's action.
One thing I know: *being blind*, now I see.	One thing I know: *although I was blind*, now I see.	Concession: The participle expresses a *concession* for the verb's action.
At the proper time, we will reap, *not giving up*.	At the proper time, we will reap *if we do not give up*.	Condition: The participle expresses a *condition* for the verb's action.
You no longer permit him to do anything for his father or mother, *making void* the word of God by your tradition.	You no longer permit him to do anything for his father or mother *with the result that you are making void* the word of God by your tradition.	Result: The participle expresses a *result* of the verb's action.
An Ethiopian eunuch had come to Jerusalem *worshiping*.	An Ethiopian eunuch had come to Jerusalem *for the purpose of worshiping* (or *in order to worship*).	Purpose: The participle expresses a *purpose* for which the verb's action occurs.

Rule 20. Don't confuse "which" and "that."[75]

Professors don't want to go on a "which hunt" through your paper to mark every time you misuse *which* and *that*. Figure 10 illustrates incorrect and correct ways to use *which* and *that*.

Fig. 10. Which vs. That

Incorrect	Correct
Roe v. Wade which became law in 1973 made it legal to murder unborn children.	*Roe v. Wade*, which became law in 1973, made it legal to murder unborn children.
This document is the manuscript which I submitted to the publisher.	This document is the manuscript that I submitted to the publisher.
My phone, that used to belong to my mom, is almost obsolete.	My phone, which used to belong to my mom, is almost obsolete.
The book which is in my hand is a classic.	The book that is in my hand is a classic.

Here's the rule:

- Use *which* when a phrase needs commas—when the phrase is *unnecessary* for the sentence to be accurate. The *which*-phrase is nonrestrictive or nondefining or parenthetical.

- Use *that* when a phrase should not have commas—when the phrase is *necessary* for the sentence to be accurate. The *that*-phrase is restrictive or defining.

Warning: British writers do not follow this rule, so don't imitate them. They use *which* and *that* interchangeably.

---

[75] Cf. *Chicago Manual of Style*, §5.254 (pp. 367–68), §6.29 (p. 392).

This rule explains the reason for including or omitting commas in Fig. 10 above:

- *Include* commas around *which*. A *which*-phrase is unnecessary for the sentence to be accurate.

- *Omit* commas around *that*. A *that*-phrase is necessary for the sentence to be accurate.

Rule 21. Don't say, "The reason why is because."

"The reason why is because" is redundant. Simply say, "The reason is that" or "The reason is."

- avoid: The reason why is because Jesus is God.
- better: The reason is that Jesus is God.

"The reason is that" is more formal than saying, "The reason is" (without the word *that*). It is clearer to include the word *that* in writing. Including the word *that* is not as crucial to include in speech.

Rule 22. Write in the present tense when discussing literature and arguments.

This is a standard convention for the humanities.

- wrong: Paul *said* that an overseer must be above reproach.
- right: Paul *says* that an overseer must be above reproach.

This rule applies to how you refer to what you write in your paper. Don't say what you will argue (future tense) in the introduction and then say what you argued (past tense) in the conclusion.

- Avoid this in the introduction: "This paper *will address* the doctrine of Scripture" (future tense).
- Avoid this in the conclusion: "This paper *addressed* the doctrine of Scripture" (past tense).
- It is better to say in both places, "This paper *addresses* the doctrine of Scripture" (present tense).

Rule 23. Don't disregard an idea simply because it is "problematic."

People often use the word *problematic* vaguely. They may apply that label to an idea as a way to discount it without giving clear reasons against the idea.

Problematic derives from *problematical*, which Noah Webster's *American Dictionary of the English Language* (1st ed., 1828) defines as "questionable; uncertain; unsettled; disputable; doubtful."

The word *problematic* has become increasingly popular in recent years and is now a catch-all term to label an idea as bad (see Fig. 11).

Fig. 11. Usage of *Problematic* from 1800 to 2022[76]

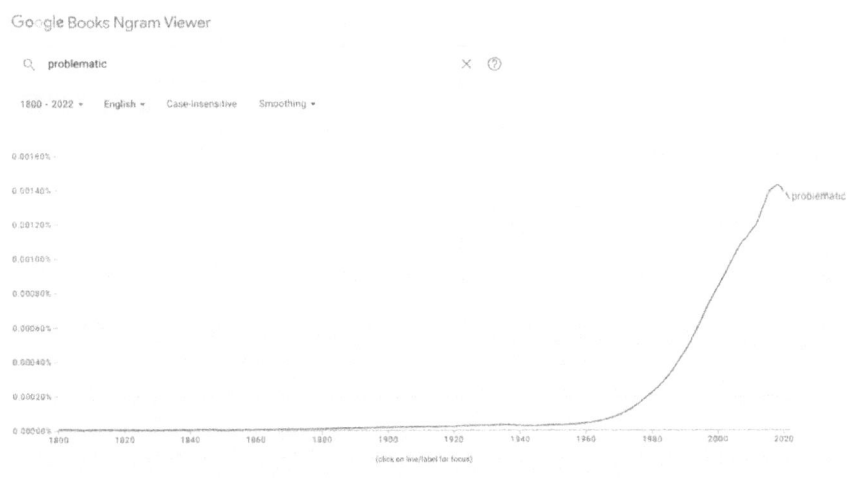

---

[76] https://books.google.com/ngrams/graph?content=problematic&year_start=1800&year_end=2022&corpus=en&smoothing=3, search on 25 July 2025.

The word *problematic* describes something that presents a problem or difficulty—something that seems doubtful or questionable or at least difficult, perplexing, puzzling, or paradoxical. In one sense, *problematic* can describe what the Bible teaches about the Trinity and the person of Christ and the problem of evil. Why? Because those teachings are *not easy*. They are *difficult*.

But that is not how most people use the word *problematic* now. Today a person uses *problematic* typically to describe *what he suspects is wrong*. It has become common for people to describe an idea as *problematic* as a way to imply that the idea is inherently wrong but without clearly explaining why. It's an easy way to place a dark cloud of suspicion over a person or idea without articulating substantial reasons.

In the past decade or so, I have noticed a trend for some left-leaning, woke-friendly people to use *problematic* as a way to write off certain people and ideas as inherently racist or homophobic or misogynistic or whatever. If you suspect that an idea is wrong, don't disregard it simply by labeling it *problematic*. Instead, explain why you think the idea is wrong.

Rule 24. An outline must have at least two headings for each level.
If you have a "I," then you need a "II."
If you have an "A," then you need a "B."
If you have a "1," then you need a "2."

Step 5. Revise:
Polish the cannonball.

When I would take exams in college, I would typically finish early and then use the remaining time to check my work. One of my professors, an officer who commanded a submarine in the Navy, referred to that as "polishing the cannonball." I like that metaphor. But it might be a bit misleading to use it for the final stage of revising a research paper because this stage often involves a lot more work than polishing a basically ready-to-go product. It may involve significant restructuring and rewriting.

> Writing is hard work. A clear sentence is no accident. Very few sentences come out right the first time, or even the third time. Remember this in moments of despair. If you find that writing is hard, it's because it *is* hard…. Rewriting is the essence of writing well: it's where the game is won or lost.[77]

Revising is crucial for writing well, and you can't complete it unless you work ahead (Step 2!). So don't procrastinate.

Here are two strategies for revising your research paper.

Strategy 1. Solicit feedback.

When I write a book or article for publication, I solicit feedback from a wide variety of people—spanning from experts with formal theological training to those with no formal training at all. I prefer to receive constructive criticism *before* my book or article is published because it strengthens the final product.

In recent years I have been drafting books and articles in Google Docs so that I can receive feedback efficiently. I invite friends to be a "Commenter" on a document online so that any update they make

---

[77] Zinsser, *On Writing Well*, 9, 83 (italics in original).

to the document is a suggestion that I can accept or decline. As I update a document in real time, there's no need for me to recontact friends with an updated draft of my document attached to an email.

You may choose to pay someone with editorial gifts to proofread your research paper. Some libraries offer proofreading services.[78] If you receive expert feedback like that, make sure you understand the reason for every update you make to your paper. This is a good way to improve at writing a research paper.

Strategy 2. Read your paper aloud to help you refine how you argue and to improve your grammar and style.

I suggest doing this in a variety of ways:

- Read your research paper aloud from your computer screen.

- Print your research paper, and read it aloud from the printed page. You may notice errors on a printed page that you miss on a screen.

- Make your computer read your research paper aloud and follow along with both your eyes and ears.

Involve as many senses as you can in this process. Your ears may hear errors that your eyes miss.

---

[78] For example, the Bethlehem College and Seminary library offers to proofread papers for our students.

Appendix A. Plagiarism:
What is it, and how can you avoid it?

The *Oxford English Dictionary* defines *plagiarism* as "the action or practice of taking someone else's work, idea, etc., and passing it off as one's own; literary theft."[79] You shouldn't present specific arguments that aren't original to you as if they are.

Often when students plagiarize material to some degree, they don't intend to. It's important to understand what plagiarism is so that you don't do it.

The standard for plagiarism in a research paper is even higher than it is for a sermon.[80] It would be annoying to listen to a sermon that verbally footnotes everything. But even for a sermon, it would be wrong to steal the wording of others. I agree with D. A. Carson:

> Taking over another sermon and preaching it as if it were yours is always and unequivocally wrong, and if you do it you should resign or be fired immediately. The wickedness is along at least three axes: (1) You are stealing. (2) You are deceiving the people to whom you are preaching. (3) Perhaps worst, you are not devoting yourself to the study of the Bible to the end that God's truth captures you, molds you, makes you a man of God and equips you to speak for him.[81]

If that's the case for a sermon, how much more is that the case for a research paper?

---

[79] https://www.oed.com/dictionary/plagiarism_n.

[80] On plagiarism and preachers, see David Schrock, *Brothers, We Are Not Plagiarists: A Pastoral Plea to Forsake the Peddling of God's Word* (Cape Coral, FL: Founders, 2022).

[81] Don Carson, "TGC Asks Don Carson: When Has a Preacher Crossed the Line into Plagiarism in His Sermon?," *The Gospel Coalition*, 16 June 2017, https://www.thegospelcoalition.org/article/tgc-asks-don-carson-when-has-a-preacher-crossed-the-line-into-plagiarism-in/.

In 2015 I asked questions about plagiarism to Justin Taylor, the executive vice president of book publishing and book publisher for Crossway.[82] I asked him four questions, and here's how he responded:

Question 1. What is plagiarism?

Plagiarism involves using the original and specific wording or arguments of others without acknowledging the source, thus giving the impression that they are original with you.

Question 2. Is plagiarism sinful?

In most cases, especially in the culture and context of the contemporary Western world, the answer is Yes. When done deliberately, I believe plagiarism is sin—even if you don't know that it is sin. It is an act of …

- theft (you have stolen someone else's intellectual property),
- deception (you have given the impression that you have created something you did not),
- pride (you want to get credit for something for which you do not deserve credit),
- harm to neighbor (you don't want someone else to get credit for something for which they deserve credit), and
- laziness (you have not done the harder work of producing original material or acknowledging where your material came from).

---

[82] Andrew David Naselli, "On Plagiarism: An Interview with Justin Taylor," *Andy Naselli*, 11 December 2015, https://andynaselli.com/on-plagiarism-an-interview-with-justin-taylor.

But we can go too far with this accusation. Plagiarism is not always black and white (there can be gray areas), and some errors are unintentional mistakes (a footnote can be accidentally deleted, for example).

There are also, I suppose, cultural and contextual factors to consider. If I am giving a devotional to my family at Christmas, it would be highly distracting to cite the sources for every point I might wish to make. And yet even there, I would not read a John Piper quote and pass it off as my own.

Question 3. How do I prevent plagiarism?

The first step is to *use common sense*. We can unnecessarily fixate on the gray areas and lose sight of the big, clear principles. When I worked for John Piper, I once discovered online (!) a pastor's sermon manuscript that was virtually verbatim from Piper's. He changed only things like "the beautiful Minnesota sunset" to "the beautiful California sunset"! He humbly repented when confronted, and he explained that this is what he was taught to do in Bible College, but I still can't help but think he had to know deep down this was wrong and deceptive.

Second, *if you copy exact wording into your notes, you have to put it in quotes and include a reference*. The reason I say "notes" here and not "final version" is that many of the unintentional problems occur because a writer might go back to old notes and not realize it was actually from someone else.

Third, *develop the habit of including in your work only quotes that are especially memorable or incisive*. Many students (and authors) are prone to include too many quotations.

Fourth, *remember that common knowledge doesn't need a citation*. The Purdue University English Department helpfully suggests that you can tell something is "common knowledge" when (1) you see it undocumented in at least five other sources, (2) you think it's something your readers will already know, or (3) you think it's something your readers can easily discover using general reference works. So, for example, the sentence "C. S. Lewis was born in Belfast, Ireland, on November 29, 1898" is in the category of "common knowledge"—and really, there are only so many ways to express this fact, and it does not need a citation. Saying that Martyn Lloyd-Jones was a powerful preacher does not need a citation. But if I said, "In the pulpit he was a lion, fierce on matters of principle, austere in his gravity, able in his prime to growl and to roar as his argument required"— I would need to show you that it was J. I. Packer who first said that, not me.

Finally, *take the small amount of time to do a little reading on plagiarism, how to cite sources, etc.* (You could start with www.plagiarism.org.) Remember that ignorance is not an excuse and that failure in this area can lead to failing a course, being dismissed from a school, getting fired from a job, and other unpleasant consequences.

Question 4. You tweeted, "Booth is wrong about exact wording of dictionary definitions being excluded from plagiarism." And you say above, "Common knowledge doesn't need a citation." How do you harmonize those statements?

The problem is using exact and specific language and syntax without attribution. For example, conceptually the definition of bulverism and its origin may be "common knowledge" (though actually I doubt it!), but if you quote the exact words from a dictionary without indicating that, then you are giving the appearance that these are your words. If it's common knowledge, why would you need to copy and paste the exact wording? Why couldn't you define it in your own words?

If I say that an apple is a fruit that grows on a tree, with red skin on the outside and a core on the inside, I've expressed a common-knowledge definition (I wrote it off the top of my head). But if I say an apple is "the round fruit of a tree of the rose family, which typically has thin red or green skin and crisp flesh," then I am relying upon a more technical formulation that someone else wrote, and I should acknowledge it as such.

Perhaps this question is a good test case: Is it possible that someone could read your definition and then cite you as the person who originally wrote that definition? You could solve most of the problems by rewriting or paraphrasing rather than copying and pasting.

I agree with C. S. Lewis: "What staggers me is how any man can prefer the galley-slave labour of transcription to the freeman's work of attempting an essay on his own."[83]

---

[83] Lewis, *The Collected Letters of C. S. Lewis*, 3:1107.

Appendix B. Artificial Intelligence:
May you use AI at any stage of the paper-writing process?

Throughout this book on how to write a paper, I give advice about matters I have thought about for decades. This appendix is the exception. I have been thinking about artificial intelligence and research papers for just a few years, and this appendix is my first attempt to suggest how to navigate this new terrain.

So may you use AI at any stage of the paper-writing process? I'll work up to that question by answering five other questions first. Then I'll answer some follow-up questions.

Question 1. Can AI write a research paper that would earn a passing grade? (Yes.)

Talking about AI right now is kind of like talking about a smartphone in 2009. (The first iPhone released in 2007.) The AI revolution is just beginning. Now that more and more people are using chatbots like ChatGPT and Grok, it is becoming increasingly obvious that AI is a big deal. AI is now mainstream. Soon most computing devices and apps and operating systems will incorporate AI.

The rise of chatbots like ChatGPT and Grok adds new temptations to writing a research paper because a student can type a specific prompt into a chatbot and generate a passable paper in a matter of seconds. I wrote this prompt for Grok in July 2025:

> Write a theological research paper with the following criteria: address the topic of what the whole Bible teaches about the destiny of infants when they die. The paper should be academic at the graduate-school level; it should be in the simple and elegant style of C. S. Lewis combined with the clarity and precision of D. A. Carson; it should be 4,000 to

5,000 words in length (including footnotes); it should be written from the perspective of a Calvinist who is a theologically conservative Protestant evangelical; it should not sound like a sermon, but it should have a pastoral tone and not sound like a heartless machine. The conclusion should be that we can't know for certain whether infants who die go to heaven but that the most likely answer is that they do go to heaven. Write in a format and style consistent with the SBL Handbook of Style, 2nd ed.

After about 90 seconds, Grok prepared a decent research paper. It is impeccably formatted. It cites some quality sources (though the page numbers are way too large for some of the sources—at this early stage, AI sometimes fabricates academic references). The organization is coherent, and the English style is better than average. If a student wrote this paper, he would definitely earn a passing grade—probably a B. That is astonishing.

Question 2. So should students no longer write research papers? (No.)

In the introduction to this book, I unpack seven benefits of writing a research paper:

1. You can think more clearly and deeply.
2. You can communicate more clearly and concisely.
3. You can more fairly evaluate opposing arguments.
4. You can better affirm and love what is true, good, and beautiful, and you can better refute and hate what is false, evil, and ugly.
5. You can better influence others.
6. You can better cultivate the virtue of self-control.
7. You can more faithfully steward the skills God has entrusted to you.

Those benefits are so valuable that students should continue to write research papers. We should not discard the paper-writing process.

Many people disagree. They basically reason like this: *Because AI can write a decent research paper, students should no longer have to write research papers.*[84] That's silly logic. Consider that same reasoning applied to other areas:

- *Because word processors make writing faster, children should no longer learn how to write by hand.* Writing by hand is a valuable and rewarding skill. It's good to master handwriting before learning to type on word processors.

- *Because a GPS device like Google Maps can give you instant step-by-step directions, young people should no longer learn how to navigate manually by reading a map.* Think about what GPS has done to many of our brains. Many people have no sense of direction, and they don't know how to read a map. They get into their car, set up the GPS on their phone, and off they go without thinking about north, south, east, or west—ever. If their phone battery dies or if they lose cell phone service, they are in big trouble because they don't know how to get anywhere without GPS. It's good to understand how to read a map before relying on GPS to navigate from point A to point B.

- *Because you can split wood with a log splitter, you should no longer use a maul to split wood.* But are there no advantages to knowing how to use a maul to split wood?

---

[84] Cf. Hua Hsu, "What Happens After A.I. Destroys College Writing?," *The New Yorker*, 30 June 2025, https://www.newyorker.com/magazine/2025/07/07/the-end-of-the-english-paper. Here's how *The New Yorker* summarizes that article in a sentence: "The demise of the English paper will end a long intellectual tradition, but it's also an opportunity to reëxamine the purpose of higher education."

What if you don't have access to a log splitter? What if you want to split only a single small log? What if you'd like to get some exercise, warm up a bit in the winter cold, and not spend money to put gas in a log splitter?

- *Because you can purchase pre-made meals and use robotic kitchen appliances, you shouldn't learn how to cook manually.* What if you can manually cook a meal that tastes better? What if it is less expensive and more enjoyable to manually cook a meal?

The logic seems to be this: *Because a machine can do it, you shouldn't have to do it.* That logic could lead you to become more and more like one of those pitiful people in the Pixar film *WALL-E* (2008).

Question 3. Do you want to become like one of those pitiful people in the movie WALL-E? (I hope not.)

Those pitiful people in the movie *WALL-E* live aboard the spaceship Axiom. They have lived in a fully automated environment for centuries, and they have become so dependent on automated technology that they are basically useless blobs:

- *They are physically obese with atrophied muscles.* They are so weak that they can't even walk. Instead of chewing food, they sip on straws. They are unable to do any manual labor. They have no self-discipline. They are slothful.

- *They are intellectually incompetent.* They are oblivious to their surroundings as they stare at a screen immediately in front of their faces. They are unable to think critically.

- *They are socially isolated.* Even though other people are all around them, each person is essentially on his own island.

The danger of over-relying on AI is that people may become more and more like *that.* They will not become better people overall. They will become less capable, less intelligent, less human.

There is a huge danger to relying too heavily on machines: *You can lose valuable abilities.* You can become flabby and out of shape physically and mentally and socially.[85]

Question 4. If AI is so dangerous, then should we avoid using it at all? (Not necessarily.)

Simply because something is dangerous does not mean that we should completely avoid it:

---

[85] Some academics argue that significant atrophy occurred well *before* AI came on the scene. For example, when T. David Gordon laments the poor quality of preaching in a book he drafted in 2004, he concludes, "The problem is the condition of the typical ministerial candidate when he *arrives* at seminary. The culture has profoundly changed since the 1950s. A culture formerly dominated by language (reading and writing) has become a culture dominated by images, even moving images.... Our seminary curricula are largely identical to what they were around the First World War, but the entering seminarian is a profoundly different person than was the seminarian of the early twentieth century. Then, the individual was well read in poetry, and had studied nearly a decade of classical language (Latin, Greek, or both), learning by reading poetry and ancient languages to read texts carefully. He had written compositions almost weekly in many of his academic classes, and often wrote letters to friends and family. In contrast, the entering seminarian today has the faculties of a sixth- to eighth-grader sixty years ago, and the seminary curriculum cannot make this seminarian an adult by the time he graduates." T. David Gordon, *Why Johnny Can't Preach: The Media Have Shaped the Messengers* (Phillipsburg, NJ: P&R Publishing, 2009), 35, 68, italics original. See, for example, an intermediate examination that Professor A. T. Robertson gave his Greek students at The Southern Baptist Theological Seminary in 1894: https://repository.sbts.edu/handle/10392/7530. Many students today whom we consider *advanced* in their Greek skills couldn't pass that exam.

- *Fire* is dangerous. It can burn your home down. But if you use it responsibly, it can heat your home during a Minnesota winter.

- *Sex* is dangerous. Sex outside of marriage is reckless, hell-deserving behavior. But if you use sex responsibly, you can honor God by filling the earth with more people who are made in his image.

- *Speed* is dangerous. If you crash while driving 70mph, your injury will be far more severe than if you tripped on a little branch while walking down the road. But if you use speed responsibly, you can travel much faster by bike or car or train or plane or rocket.

- *Alcohol* is dangerous. It can make you drunk, but if you use it responsibly, you can enjoy it to the glory of God as it gladdens your heart.

- *Weapons* are dangerous. A gun or knife could be a tool to murder someone. But if you use a gun or knife responsibly, you could provide food for your family or defend innocent women and children.

- *Money and possessions* are dangerous. In Jesus's parable of the sower, he explains the third kind of soil: "As for what was sown among thorns, this is the one who hears the word, but the cares of the world and the deceitfulness of riches choke the word, and it proves unfruitful" (Matt 13:22). Money and possessions can choke you to death (see also Mark 10:23, 25; 1 Tim 6:9–10). But money and possessions are not inherently evil. The problem is when you *love* money. You should enjoy money and possessions as gifts from God (Eccl 5:19; 1 Tim 4:1–5; 6:17).

- *Tools* are dangerous. A chainsaw or tablesaw or tractor is so powerful that it could seriously injure you or even kill you. But if you use such tools responsibly, you could cut wood and transport loads and till the ground far better than you could without such tools.

AI is similar. It is dangerous, but you can use it responsibly.

Question 5. How can you use AI responsibly? (With caution.)

It is possible to use AI as a tool for the glory of God.[86] Since AI is dangerous, you must be intentional to use it carefully. I'm not an expert on AI, and I've been cautious about using it. As I draft this appendix on AI, I have been using an AI chatbot for over a year. It's amazing. Here are some practical ways that I have attempted to use AI responsibly:

1. *Verify facts.* AI is a quick way to cross-check facts. (As you do, ask AI for *sources* to confirm that it's not making stuff up.) For example, on July 7, 2025, I saw a news report on X that starting that day, the TSA was removing its twenty-year-old shoe-removal rule for passengers at airports. I quickly confirmed this fact with AI and learned that it stems from advances in screening technology, which detects over 99% of concealed explosives.

2. *Keep sensitive personal and confidential data secure.* Assume that anything you upload into a chatbot is not secure.

3. *Disclose when you use AI.* If I create content with AI and share that content with others, I tell them that it's AI-

---

[86] Cf. Thomas Dodds, "Use AI For the Sake of Good Work," *Christ Over All*, 27 May 2024, https://christoverall.com/article/concise/use-ai-for-the-sake-of-good-work/.

generated. For example, I was trying to figure out how to purchase a car from out of state and get new license plates in a way that follows state regulations, and I copied and pasted AI's answer and shared it with someone else *as AI's answer*.

4. *Treat AI like an old Google search.* I prefer to search AI instead of how I used to search Google-like search engines. AI searches save me time by organizing the search results and giving me more complete answers (with links to sources).

5. *Search for the source and precise wording of a quotation.* I love this feature. It really is remarkable. Sometimes I know that a particular person said something, but I can't remember exactly what or exactly where. I can usually locate it by typing the gist of the quote into an AI chatbot. (I did that earlier in this book for Tolkien's leaf-mold quote in Step 2.)

6. *Condense and simplify a long and complicated document.* You can upload a long medical report or a transcript or a tax code or a city's code of ordinances or a Supreme Court opinion or a medical insurance document. Then you can ask specific questions about it to try to understand it more accurately.

7. *Ask for step-by-step instructions for fixing or troubleshooting devices in your home.* How do you make your daughter's wrist watch stop beeping every hour on the hour? How do you troubleshoot the hot water heater in your home? How do you install a particular toilet fill valve model in a toilet tank?

This is a key principle for how to use AI with caution: *Use AI to access specific information, not to create content that you use to plagiarize*.

Question 6. So may you use AI in the paper-writing process? (Yes, but with strict conditions.)

My close friend Phil Gons is Chief Product Officer for Logos. Logos makes Logos Bible Software, which has recently been incorporating AI into its product. In June 2025, Gons gave a presentation on AI in which he insightfully proposed four different ways of using AI:[87]

1. Discover: Find and consume relevant content. *AI retrieves; you research and write.*

2. Ideate: Ideate and dialog to get started. *AI kickstarts; you write and finish.*

3. Refine: Refine content you've produced. *You write; AI finishes.*

4. Generate: Produce content to refine. *AI writes; you finish.*

I'll refer to those four ways of using AI in what follows.

So may you use AI in the paper-writing process? Here's the answer *for my students*: You may use AI for some of the paper-writing process but only on the following four conditions.

Condition 1. You may use AI to help you discover content.

In other words, Gons's first way of using AI is permissible: "Discover: Find and consume relevant content. *AI retrieves; you*

---

[87] Phil Gons links to the slides of this presentation in this article: Phil Gons, "AI in Christian Higher Education," *Phil Gons*, 19 July 2025, https://philgons.com/2025/07/ai-in-christian-higher-education/.

research and write." For example, you might ask if there are any other specific academic resources you should engage—such as a resource in favor or against the thesis you are defending in your paper. When you use AI to assist you with research, it is basically a more advanced search than a Google search.

Condition 2. You may not use AI at all for the hard work of writing.

In other words, Gons's final three ways of using AI are *not* permissible:

2. Ideate: Ideate and dialog to get started. *AI kickstarts; you write and finish.*

3. Refine: Refine content you've produced. *You write; AI finishes.*

4. Generate: Produce content to refine. *AI writes; you finish.*

A student might object, "I understand why you prohibit using AI to *refine* or *generate* content. Otherwise I won't increase my skill at writing well, and I might be tempted not to write original thoughts. But using AI to *ideate* is different. I find it helpful to use AI as a conversation partner." In reply, I recognize that it might be valuable to use AI as a conversation partner.[88] But I am forbidding that use because I want my students to develop specific skills in research and

---

[88] E.g., Phil Gons wrote this to me in an email: "I've found *AI as a conversation partner* to be a really helpful way to organize, sharpen, and refine my thinking. Ideally, we'd do that work with a human thought partner. I don't love how AI gives the illusion of being human. There's risk here, in my opinion, especially for the immature and vulnerable. But I'm not sure it crosses a line—at least for the mature who can remind themselves that machines are not made in God's image. But having a conversation is very open-ended and could quickly verge from helpful into questionable—especially as you drift away from *inputs to you* and toward *outputs for you*" (email from Phil Gons to Andy Naselli, 12 July 2025, shared with permission).

writing. Yes, you could ride an electric bike up a hill, and that might be valuable in some circumstances. But in this circumstance in which I am *training* students, I require a student to pedal up the hill manually.

Condition 3. You may use AI to assist you with copy-editing.

You may benefit from AI helping you spot errors in your grammar, style, and format (e.g., a chatbot, an AI-powered extension like Grammarly, or a built-in AI tool in Word or Google Docs). But you may not do this as a bulk edit that automatically makes changes without you interacting and learning about every single update. You must manually make each change yourself in your text document, and as you do so you must understand the reason for each update you make. That will help you learn and improve.

Again, you may *not* use AI to write your paper in any sense. It's cheating to use AI to draft any part of your paper and then for you to tweak it a bit in your own wording and style. AI must not replace *original thinking* and *original writing*.

Condition 4. You must disclose how you used AI.

If you use AI, then you must answer the following questions when you submit your paper:

1. What AI tools did you use? (E.g., ChatGPT, Grok, Logos AI.)

2. How did you use AI? (E.g., to discover content, to assist with copy-editing.)

3. If you used a chatbot, then what prompts did you enter? List every search/command you entered into an AI chatbot as you worked on your paper.[89]

4. Did you use AI to produce any of the content in your paper such as its structure, arguments, or wording— whether quoting or paraphrasing? (The correct answer is No.)

Question 7. Why are the conditions for using AI so strict? (To avoid the sin of plagiarism and to help you increase your skill at writing a paper.)

The obvious reason is my conditions for using AI are so strict is that *you must not plagiarize*. It's very easy to plagiarize with AI, and plagiarism is a sin. Again, see Appendix A.

Another reason is positive: It's to help you get stronger!

If you want the benefits of strength training, then you have to work hard at strength training. There are no shortcuts. Somebody else can't lift weights on your behalf. Sure, a fork lift can pick up heavy objects, but if *you* want to get stronger, then *you* must do the work.

If you want the benefits of paper writing, then you have to work hard at the whole process of writing a research paper. There are no shortcuts. Sure, AI can write a decent paper, but if *you* want to get stronger overall as a person, then *you* must do the work. If you use

---

[89] One of my friends offered me some friendly pushback about this rule: "I think this misunderstands how people actually use AI productively. It's not like doing Google searches. It's more conversational. You might have a 50+ exchange conversation that goes down rabbit trails, circles back, and explores dead ends. Requiring students to document all of that would be like asking them to transcribe every conversation they have about their topic. It would probably discourage the thoughtful, exploratory use that could actually enhance their learning." I may revise my policy at some point down the road, but for now I like how this policy discourages students from heavily using AI.

AI to automate learning, then you won't actually learn. As tech journalist Nicholas Carr says, "You get this illusion of thinking you know something without going through the hard work of actually learning it."[90]

Using AI to cheat in any form is hurting yourself. I recently saw a video taken inside a fitness center where a personal trainer is working with a client. The trainer instructs the client to do walking lunges with dumbbells in each hand. The client is supposed to do walking lunges across the room and then turn around and do walking lunges back. As the client begins her lunges, she notices that the trainer turns his back to her as he talks with someone else. While the trainer's back is turned to her, she stops lunging to each knee and instead walks quickly to the other side of the room and turns around. She thinks she is being clever to cheat like that. But the joke is on her. She is paying her trainer good money to help her get stronger, and she is spending her valuable time in the gym. But instead of following her trainer's plan, she is cheating. She is wasting money and wasting time.

Student, if you cheat on your research paper, the joke is on you. You are paying good money and devoting your valuable time to get an education, so you are defrauding yourself. Or if someone else is graciously paying for your education, then you are defrauding that benefactor. Instead of becoming a better all-around person, you are cheating. And when you cheat like that, you are dishonoring God, not loving your neighbor, and hurting yourself.

Question 8. Can professors enforce such rules against using AI? (Not infallibly.)

It's impossible for professors to catch students every time they cheat by using AI to write a paper. We can run the papers through

---

[90] Cited in Janie B. Cheaney, "Truth and Technology," *WORLD*, 9 July 2025, https://wng.org/podcasts/janie-b-cheaney-truth-and-technology-1751992461.

software that detects plagiarism. We can pay attention to how a student tends to communicate in speech and in writing and then see if we notice a discrepancy in how he wrote a paper. (At my school if we discover that a student is guilty of substantial plagiarism, the penalty is severe: The student immediately receives a failing grade for the course, and the school places the student on probation.)

But professors are not infallible at detecting plagiarism. So here's what it comes down to, dear student: Someday you are going to stand before God and give an account for everything you have done. That includes whether you use AI to cheat on your research papers. So for the glory of God and for the good of your soul and to keep a clean conscience, don't plagiarize.

Appendix C. Grading Rubric:
What is a fair and reasonable way to grade a research paper?

There is not a universal standard for grading a research paper. It's challenging to give a specific number grade like 87/100 for a paper. Grading a paper is partly subjective. It's not like grading a multiple-choice exam or a true-false quiz. But it's still possible to assign a fair and reasonable grade to a research paper. I do it by using the following grading rubric.[91] These criteria help make grading a research paper a little more objective. I've been using this grading rubric since about 2014, and I think it works well. It's based on a 10-point scale:

94–100 A
90–93   A-

87–89   B+
84–86   B
80–83   B-

77–79   C+
74–76   C
70–73   C-

67–69   D+
64–66   D
60–63   D-

0–59   F

---

[91] I adapted this from Mark Boda, "Designing and Evaluating Learning Experiences for Courses," in *Those Who Can, Teach: Teaching as Christian Vocation*, ed. Stanley E. Porter, McMaster General Series 3 (Eugene, OR: Pickwick, 2013), 87.

Fig. 12. A Grading Rubric

Grade Range	Content (40%)	Argument (40%)	Presentation (20%)
A, A-	• Mastery • Score: 36–40	• Clear • Logical • Comprehensive • Critical • Innovative • Persuasive • Score: 36–40	• Almost no errors in format (front matter, headers, body text, footnotes, bibliography), grammar, and syntax • Elegant • Within the word count • Score: 18–20
B+, B, B-	• Above-average grasp • Score: 32–35	• Coherent • Well-stated • Score: 32–35	• Several errors in format, grammar, and syntax • Score: 16–17
C+, C, C-	• Adequate grasp • Score: 28–31	• Marginally coherent • Rudimentary • Minimal • Score: 28–31	• Significant errors in format, grammar, and syntax • Score: 14–15

Grade Range	Content (40%)	Argument (40%)	Presentation (20%)
D+, D, D-	• Low-level grasp • Score: 24–27	• Incoherent • Illogical • Score: 24–27	• Abundant errors in format, grammar, and syntax • Score: 12–13
F	• Little-to-no grasp: fails to grasp basic concepts and omits required elements • Score: 0–23	• Incomprehensible • Extremely illogical • Score: 0–23	• Egregious errors in format, grammar, and syntax • Score: 0–11
Score	__/40	__/40	__/20
Overall Grade: __/100			

Appendix D. Productivity:
How should you manage your time so that you can write a good research paper?[92]

Before I suggest some tips, I'll ask some diagnostic questions to help you calibrate how to think about managing your time.

Question 1. How well are you doing right now?

If you came to me for advice about how to use your time more productively, I might ask you to write out everything you did in the past week in at least 15-minute increments. How much time did you spend sleeping? Playing video games? Watching videos? Scrolling social media? Checking email? Texting? When you list everything honestly, you may be embarrassed at how you use your time.

As a general rule, you find time to do what you most want to do. Are you wisely stewarding the time God gives you?

Fig. 13. Time-Management Grid

	Urgent	**Not Urgent**
Important	1. Important + urgent (immediate and important deadlines)	2. Important + not urgent (long-term strategies and development)
Not Important	3. Not important + urgent (time-pressured distractions)	4. Not important + not urgent (what you might do when taking a break from urgent and important activities)

---

[92] This appendix updates Naselli, *How to Read a Book*, 139–41.

It's common for literature on productivity to present a four-quadrant time-management grid (see Fig. 13).[93] If you are typical, then you *want* to spend more time in quadrant 2 (important and not urgent), but you actually spend most time in quadrants 1 and 3 (urgent). What is urgent dictates what you do. When you feel pressured to complete urgent tasks, that tempts you to unwind by escaping to quadrant 4 (not important and not urgent). Perhaps you fritter away time by consuming social media candy—a cat video, a feel-good news story, so-called "breaking news" about a celebrity you don't really care about.[94]

Social media can be like a magnet in quadrant 4 that constantly pulls you in and keeps you longer than you want to stay. Tristan Harris, who served as a Design Ethicist for Google from 2013 to 2016, says that social media intentionally exploits "our minds' weaknesses" and plays "your psychological vulnerabilities (consciously and unconsciously) against you in the race to grab your attention."[95]

Since you tend to do what's urgent (quadrants 1 and 3) or what's neither urgent nor important (quadrant 4), productivity gurus emphasize that you should first do what is important and not urgent (quadrant 2). Stephen Covey often demonstrated this in seminars by placing a large clear cylinder on a table along with some big rocks,

---

[93] E.g., Stephen R. Covey, *The 7 Habits of Highly Effective People: Powerful Lessons in Personal Change*, 3rd ed. (New York: Simon & Schuster, 2013), 159–89.

[94] Cf. Tony Reinke, "Six Wrong Reasons to Check Your Phone in the Morning: And a Better Way Forward," Desiring God, 6 June 2015, http://www.desiringgod.org/articles/six-wrong-reasons-to-check-your-phone-in-the-morning.

[95] Tristan Harris, "How Technology Hijacks People's Minds—from a Magician and Google's Design Ethicist," *The Startup*, May 18, 2016, https://medium.com/swlh/how-technology-hijacks-peoples-minds-from-a-magician-and-google-s-design-ethicist-56d62ef5edf3#.gmdbv6oe5. See "Appendix 3: Why and How I Use Social Media" in Naselli, *How to Read a Book*, 175–89.

medium-sized rocks, little rocks, and sand.[96] The big rocks represent items in quadrant 2 (important and not urgent). The only way all the items could fit in the cylinder is to put the big rocks in first and the sand in last.

Take stock of your life right now. Be brutally honest. How well are you doing at managing your time?

Question 2. How urgent and important is writing a research paper?

In the time-management grid above, writing a research paper should go in quadrant 2. It's important but not urgent:

- Writing a research paper is *important* because of all the benefits I mention in this book's introduction. Also, it's a student's responsibility to do what the professor assigns for a class.

- Writing a research paper is *not urgent* because the deadline is far away. Or at least it *should* be far away when you are starting the process to research and write the paper! (See Step 2 of this book.)

Your problem may be that the deadline for writing a research paper always seems to be *urgent* because you have failed to plan ahead. "Your other work will get done if you prioritize your writing, but your writing will not get done if you do not prioritize it."[97]

---

[96] "Big Rocks," FranklinCovey, August 24, 2017, https://www.youtube.com/watch?v=zV3gMTOEWt8.

[97] Benjamin L. Merkle and Adrianne Cheek Miles, *Christian Academic Writing: Twelve Practices and Principles for Becoming a Successful Writer* (Grand Rapids: Baker Academic, 2024), 25.

Question 3. What is a good book to help you revamp how you organize your time?

Check out Tim Challies's book *Do More Better*.[98] It's the most clear and concise book on productivity I've read. It's full of wise, practical, theologically sound advice, and I've been following it ever since I read it in 2015. Challies recommends "three essential tools":

1. *Use a task management tool to capture and organize your projects and tasks.* Challies recommends Todoist. (I agree.)

2. *Use a scheduling tool to organize your time and notify you of pending events and appointments.* Challies recommends Google Calendar. (I agree.)

3. *Use an information tool to collect, archive, and access information.* Challies recommends Evernote. (I recommend Microsoft OneNote.)

Do More Better convinced me that I should specify my main responsibilities more carefully. I can fit just about everything under three categories: personal, family, and professor-pastor. Those are my main headings in Todoist, Google Calendar, and OneNote.

Why should you take time to use tools like Todoist, Google Calendar, and OneNote? Challies nails it in this paragraph:

> I don't mean to disparage the brain. It's a remarkable organ and an outstanding evidence of the existence and wisdom of God. Yet the brain is limited in its capacity. Though the brain is perfectly capable of remembering much of life's mundane information, it is better to dedicate it to more important matters. Why focus on memorizing the details of that hotel

---

[98] Tim Challies, *Do More Better: A Practical Guide to Productivity* (Minneapolis: Cruciform, 2015).

reservation when you could put the effort into memorizing Scripture? Most of life's information can be added to your information tool. You can then trust this tool to remember it and to present it to you when you need it. This approach enables you to give your limited memory to only the most important facts and information.[99]

Question 4. What are some time-management tips for writing a good research paper?

This book presents a five-step method for writing a research paper, and Step 2 is crucial: "Plan Ahead: Prepare far in advance so that you complete your research paper well before the deadline." Here are some specific tips to incorporate as you plan ahead:

Tip 1. Get in the zone.

To get in the zone means to get absorbed in the task. It's doing "deep work."[100] To do this when you research and write, you must not get distracted. How?

- *Set aside long blocks of time to research and write.* I'm like a train. I don't accelerate quickly to my max speed, but once I get going, I make good progress. I can't do that in five-minute spurts. I work best with long, uninterrupted periods. How can you reserve blocks of time to research and write? *Enter appointments in your calendar for when you plan to research and write, and block off those times.* If someone asks if you are free to meet during that time, then you may honestly reply, "No." That's true because you have previously committed to do something else during that time.

---

[99] Challies, *Do More Better*, 67.

[100] Cf. Cal Newport, *Deep Work: Rules for Focused Success in a Distracted World* (New York: Grand Central, 2016).

- *Work in a place that is ideal for you to focus.* This might be a room in your home or an office at work or a library or a coffee shop. Where can you work with the least number of distractions?

- *Don't switch over to anything that is not directly related to research and writing.* Don't check your email or texts or social media or ESPN when it's research-and-writing time.

- *Silence all notifications on your devices.* You shouldn't be hearing a ding or feeling a vibration or seeing a notification flash on your screen every time somebody emails you or texts you or mentions you on social media. Every notification derails you and prevents you from getting in the zone.

- *Don't multitask.* "To multitask is to do two or more things at once that require mental focus. Multitasking seems like a way to save time but actually costs more time and is, in fact, impossible."[101] If you multitask while researching and writing, "You will never get into the zone. And if you never get into the zone, you will miss out on the best and most productive experience in work."[102]

Tip 2. Plod.

Sometimes researching and writing is thrilling. I get in the zone. I move along at warp speed. I lose track of what time it is. I feel like the paper-writing version of Eric Liddell, the Scottish Olympic runner who says in the movie *Chariots of Fire*, "I believe God made

---

[101] Matt Perman, *What's Best Next: How the Gospel Transforms the Way You Get Things Done* (Grand Rapids: Zondervan, 2014), 241.

[102] Matt Perman, "What's at Stake with Multitasking?," *What's Best Next*, 8 April 2009, https://www.whatsbestnext.com/2009/04/whats-at-stake-with-multitasking/.

me for a purpose, but he also made me fast. And when I run, I feel his pleasure." I don't recall ever feeling like that when I run, but I feel God's pleasure when I am in the zone researching and writing.

I love that feeling. But if I research and write *only* when I feel that way, then I wouldn't write much. The process of researching and writing involves disciplined *plodding*. To *plod* means to work slowly and perseveringly at a dull task. Don't misunderstand me. I'm not describing researching and writing as *dull*. But sometimes it can feel that way. And when it does, you must *keep plodding*. Don't wait for perfect conditions to get going.

Is it ideal to research and write during large blocks of time? Yes. But that's not the *only* time to research and write. You don't have to block off an hour or a full day or a week or a month to make progress. Some academics never get around to writing a book because they keep waiting to have the perfect conditions for getting in the zone—like a distraction-free twelve-month research sabbatical. When you have only bits of time here and there, make the best of it. This is one of D. A. Carson's "secrets of productivity": "Learn to fill in the little empty periods that clutter each day."[103] Do that *routinely*. Doug Wilson calls this *ploductivity*:

> The pace of work can be a problem two ways. One way is when the marathon runner starts out as though the race were a hundred-yard dash. Not surprisingly, he burns out after just a few minutes. Another trick, one that many learned in college by postponing the writing of the paper until the night before it was due, is the technique of walking the length of the marathon, and then bursting into a sprint for the last hundred yards. That usually doesn't work either....
>
> Methodical is what does the trick. An amazing amount of work can be accomplished through diligent plodding. But

---

[103] D. A. Carson, "Christ and the Academy: An Interview with D. A. Carson," *Ligonier Ministries*, 24 December 2012, https://learn.ligonier.org/articles/christ-and-the-academy.

please note that I said plodding, not shuffling. There is a way of dragging your feet that doesn't really accomplish anything remarkable either. But simply placing one foot in front of the other, and doing so repeatedly, can get you across a continent within a reasonable amount of time.[104]

Tip 3. Don't just sit there. Move!

When you are researching and writing for long blocks of time, it's not ideal to sit the entire time. It's not healthy to be sedentary. It's good for your body and your mind to move—even if you're simply strolling along at 1.4mph on a treadmill desk. When I research and write, I alternate between four positions: sitting, standing, walking (on a treadmill desk), and biking (on a bike desk).[105]

Tip 4. Eat well, do strength training, do cardio, and sleep 8+ hours.[106]

How does this tip connect to writing a good research paper? If you are overweight, weak, out of shape, and sleep-deprived, then your body is not firing on all cylinders. You might be running on fumes. You are more lethargic than you should be. You could feel more energetic and be more alert. You could be mentally sharper. What physical state do you think is optimal for the hard work of researching and writing?

---

[104] Douglas Wilson, *Ploductivity: A Practical Theology of Work and Wealth* (Moscow, ID: Canon, 2020), 91–92.

[105] See Andrew David Naselli, "How I Set Up My Desks: One for Sitting, One for Walking," *Andy Naselli*, 13 May 2014, https://andynaselli.com/how-i-set-up-my-desks-one-for-sitting-one-for-walking.

[106] See Andrew David Naselli, "How I Got Stronger with Strength Training (with Advice for Beginners)," *Andy Naselli*, 29 November 2023, https://andynaselli.com/how-i-got-stronger-with-strength-training-with-advice-for-beginners.

Tip 5. Use Zotero.

If you use Zotero strategically, it will save you time by helping you stay organized as you research and write. It will also save you time by helping you use the proper format for footnotes and your bibliography.[107]

Tip 6. Don't plagiarize.

Wouldn't it save time to cheat with AI? How is "Don't plagiarize" a time-saving tip? This is a time-saving tip in the *long*-term. If you are walking in the light and keeping a clear conscience before God, then you will confess your sins to God and man. So if you cheat on a research paper, then you will eventually confess that sin to God and to your professor. The consequences of that sin will be much more time-consuming than it would have been to not cheat in the first place. Don't believe the lie that plagiarizing is a legitimate option. (See Appendices A and B above.)

Tip 7. Develop a system to capture insights that come to mind when you are not researching and writing.

Some of my best ideas spontaneously come to me when I am not sitting in front of my computer to research and write. When that happens, I try to immediately capture the insight on my phone either as an audio file or in writing (usually as a new task in Todoist to process later).

---

[107] See "Appendix D: Why and How I Organize My Personal Library" in Naselli, *How to Read a Book*, 191–203.

Appendix E. The Research-and-Write Process: Two Examples

Here are examples of the process I followed to research and write two of my books: a commentary on 1 Corinthians and a book on predestination. Writing a commentary or a theology book is a more rigorous process than writing a research paper, but the principles are the same.

Example 1. A Commentary on 1 Corinthians[108]

My research-and-write process had three phases:
Phase 1: Prepare to write the commentary (2014–2017).

- I phrased 1 Corinthians. I traced the argument in the form of a phrase diagram.[109]

- I memorized 1 Corinthians.[110] It takes about an hour to read aloud.

- I taught on 1 Corinthians and sketched out notes as I did. I taught on 1 Corinthians during a semester of Sunday School for adults in my church, and I taught three seminary courses on the letter—one an intermediate Greek exegesis course and two of them ThM courses.

---

[108] Andrew David Naselli, "1 Corinthians," in *Romans–Galatians*, vol. 10 of *ESV Expository Commentary* (Wheaton, IL: Crossway, 2020), 209–394.

[109] I explain that method in chapter 5 of Andrew David Naselli, *How to Understand and Apply the New Testament: Twelve Steps from Exegesis to Theology*, 2nd ed. (Phillipsburg, NJ: P&R Publishing, 2027). The phrase diagram is now published: Andrew David Naselli, *Tracing the Argument of 1 Corinthians: A Phrase Diagram* (Bellingham, WA: Logos, 2023).

[110] Andrew David Naselli, "Why and How to Memorize an Entire Book of the Bible," *Andy Naselli*, 22 October 2015, https://andynaselli.com/why-and-how-to-memorize-an-entire-book-of-the-bible.

The notes I sketched out were invaluable for drafting the commentary more efficiently.

- I continually meditated on 1 Corinthians.

- I collected books and articles on 1 Corinthians, and I organized them in Zotero. I collected over 2,000 resources to process.

- I studied in depth parts of 1 Corinthians that I wanted to better understand. I presented three papers on 1 Corinthians at the annual meeting for the Evangelical Theological Society and turned them into articles. Here are four articles I wrote as I prepared to write the commentary:

  o "Is Every Sin Outside the Body Except Immoral Sex? Weighing Whether 1 Corinthians 6:18b Is Paul's Statement or a Corinthian Slogan." *Journal of Biblical Literature* 136 (2017): 969–87.

  o "The Structure and Theological Message of 1 Corinthians." *Presbyterion* 44.1 (2018): 98–114.

  o "Was It Always Idolatrous for Corinthian Christians to Eat Εἰδωλόθυτα in an Idol's Temple? (1 Cor 8–10)." *Southeastern Theological Review* 9 (2018): 23–45.

  o "What the New Testament Teaches About Divorce and Remarriage." *Detroit Baptist Seminary Journal* 24 (2019): 3–44.

Phase 2: Draft the commentary (January–June 2018). Bethlehem College and Seminary graciously granted me a sabbatical for the first half of 2018, which my family spent at Tyndale House in Cambridge, England. My main goal for researching and writing on that sabbatical was to draft this commentary. I had a tight word-limit (about 85,000 words), so I asked God to give me a double portion of Derek Kidner's spirit—witty brevity. This was my basic process while drafting the commentary:

- I broke the letter down into literary units, and I drafted comments on one unit at a time in order.

- I determined what resources I planned to consult for every literary section (e.g., the most helpful commentaries). I had about fifty resources in this category.

- I drafted comments on a literary unit. I did not look at secondary literature at this point. I used only the Greek NT, my phrase diagram, and English translations. I placed several English translations in parallel columns in Logos Bible Software: NASB, ESV, NIV, NIrV, CSB, NET + NET notes, and NLT. Carefully working through those English translations (including every translator's footnote and cross-reference) was as helpful as (if not more helpful than) working through secondary literature. I would add comments to my working draft when I had exegetical questions so that I could come back to those later. By the time I turned to secondary literature, I had drafted about 90% of my comments on a literary unit.

- I worked through secondary literature in Zotero—both the resources I consulted for every unit as well as other resources specific to that unit. For example, for 1 Cor 12–

14, I worked through over 600 secondary resources. I would start by working more slowly and thoroughly through the most helpful resources. After the first ten to twenty resources, it starts to snowball and go much more quickly.

- I talked to and corresponded with fellow academics all along the way to discuss exegetical and theological issues. For example, Bruce Winter—one of the top evangelical experts in the world on the historical-cultural context of Corinth—was studying at Tyndale House for a few months while I was there, and he kindly conversed with me a good deal about 1 Corinthians.

- I proofread my work and then moved on to the next section.

- I solicited feedback from a variety of friends spanning from those with no formal theological training to those with a lot of it.

Phase 3: Finalize the commentary (late 2018 to early 2020). I processed feedback from Crossway editors—first the NT editors for the commentary series (Jim Hamilton and Dane Ortlund) and then some copyeditors.

Example 2. A Book on Predestination[111]

This was the research-and-write process:

- I spent about twenty-five years studying exegesis and theology. OK, I'm being a bit facetious. But it's like when someone asks a preacher, "How long did it take you

---

[111] Andrew David Naselli, *Predestination: An Introduction*, Short Studies in Systematic Theology (Wheaton, IL: Crossway, 2024).

to write that sermon?" and he replies, "My whole life." I've been attempting to dig deep exegetical and theological wells that I can draw from. I've been repeatedly reading and memorizing and studying and meditating on the Bible—and reading and doing theology. This book builds on that foundation. In other words, I benefited from the leaf mold of my mind.

- I did word studies on every Hebrew and Greek word related to predestination. I studied each passage in its literary context, and I used multiple Bible translations (prior to consulting commentaries)—especially the NASB, ESV, NIV, NIrV, CSB, NET, and NLT.

- I located and studied every relevant passage in the Bible on predestination.

- I formed an outline for how best to answer the question "What does the whole Bible teach about predestination?"

- I drafted the book bit by bit before I turned to secondary literature.

- I collected and organized secondary literature in Zotero. I collected about 800 books and articles (not counting commentaries) and organized them in the following folders: election, reprobation, destiny of infants and mentally disabled, general systematic theology, mystery, providence, Calvinism and Arminianism, free will, problem of evil.

- I micro-read some of the most significant secondary literature, and I updated my book as I processed each item.

- I macro-read and surveyed the remaining secondary literature, and I continued to update my book. From the 800 resources I collected to work through, I created a folder of about 150 resources that I calculated would be most valuable, so I worked through those first (micro-reading and macro-reading). After that, it was downhill sledding.

- I solicited feedback from a wide variety of people—spanning from those with no formal training to experts with a lot of it. I drafted the book in Google Docs in order to receive feedback efficiently. After I drafted the book, I met in person with four groups of pastors/theologians who volunteered to read the draft and share feedback.

- I preached a four-part series on predestination to my church.

- I taught a DMin course on predestination at The Master's Seminary.

- I submitted the manuscript to Crossway.

- I processed feedback from Crossway editors.

The above two examples are for academic *books*, so the process is more rigorous than for a research paper. I share these examples to illustrate that the six components of the research-and-writing stage (Step 4 above) are interrelated throughout that process. You should be working on all six components to various degrees until you finish the draft of your research paper.

Acknowledgements

Thanks to friends for contributing to this book:

1. My professors—especially Layton Talbert and Don Carson—trained me how to research and write.

2. My dad, Charles Naselli, has made me a better writer by giving me insightful feedback on nearly everything I've written for publication—including this book.

3. Chancellor John Piper, President Brian Tabb, and other leaders of Bethlehem College and Seminary encourage and empower me to research and write.

4. Some friends and family graciously offered feedback on drafts of this book, including Scott Aniol, Andrew Ballard, Seth Beyersdorf, Josh Bremerman, Brian Collins, Josh Daws, Eddie DSouza, Phil Gons, John Hughes, Scott Jamison, Tim Miller, Charles Naselli, Kara Naselli, Layton Talbert, Josh Sullivan, Justin Taylor, Silas Tuthill, Mark Ward, Fred Zaspel, and my students in fall 2025.

Andy Naselli gives advice about how to write a paper. He breaks down the paper-writing process into five steps:

1. *Understand the assignment*. Know where you are trying to go before you start the journey.
2. *Plan ahead*. Prepare far in advance so that you complete your research paper well before the deadline.
3. *Choose your approach*. Prove a thesis (deductive), or explore a problem (inductive).
4. *Research and write*. Draft the paper.
5. *Revise*. Polish the cannonball.

Step 4 is the big one, so most of the book explains the research-and-write stage. It has six interconnected components: research, organizing the paper, developing a coherent argument, interacting with contrary views, writing clearly and concisely, using proper grammar, syntax, and format, and removing distractions by mastering the mechanics. Appendices address plagiarism, artificial intelligence, grading, and productivity.

Andy Naselli (PhD, Bob Jones University; PhD, Trinity Evangelical Divinity School) is Professor of Systematic Theology and New Testament for Bethlehem College and Seminary in Minneapolis (bcsmn.edu) and lead pastor of Christ the King Church in Stillwater, Minnesota (ChristTheKing.build). Andy and his wife, Jenni, have been married since 2004, and God has blessed them with four daughters.

 **BUILD & FIGHT PRESS**
LAKE ELMO, MINNESOTA

www.ingramcontent.com/pod-product-compliance
Lightning Source LLC
Chambersburg PA
CBHW060433130626
46555CB00005B/2341

* 9 7 9 8 9 9 4 6 4 8 0 0 1 *